Expedition
from the
Backdoor

YVETTE PRIMROSE

The Book Guild Ltd

First published in Great Britain in 2018 by
The Book Guild Ltd
9 Priory Business Park
Wistow Road, Kibworth
Leicestershire, LE8 0RX
Freephone: 0800 999 2982
www.bookguild.co.uk
Email: info@bookguild.co.uk
Twitter: @bookguild

Typeset in Adobe Garamond Pro

Printed and bound in Great Britain by CPI Group (UK) Ltd, Croydon, CR0 4YY

ISBN 978 1912362 912

British Library Cataloguing in Publication Data.
A catalogue record for this book is available from the British Library.

To Katy June Primrose.

Acknowledgements

The greatest thanks must go to my family, especially my husband Andy for mobilising his tireless forces to encourage me, tell me what I didn't want to hear, and scrape me and the book off the floor and the walls to get me working on it again. During the several years leading up to this book and including other written pieces, I've been privileged to have a father-in-law, Bob, and mother, Juliet, who have generously given many hours of intelligent attention to my drafts, yielding numerous improvements to my writing, and self-belief. The book wouldn't exist without the Expedition of course, and I could be secure in the knowledge that wherever I ended up my sister, Louise, would be there very soon to meet me and see me all right. That has, in fact, always been the case.

My publishers, The Book Guild, have been instrumental in the very completion of the book, encouraging me after a premature draft, made half way, to hold off with submission until the Expedition was completed. It was sound, and testing, advice, and I thank them for subsequently taking my book on.

I would also like to dedicate this book to SurgeryInFrance, namely Laurent Locke, and Dr Michaut, of Clinique St Roch, Toulon. Through them I gained an accurate diagnosis of necrosis of the femoral head, which left undiagnosed and untreated has led to arthritis, and now have a new ceramic hip. Thanks to them I can have an 'expeditionary' future.

The Author

I was born in 1966, in Plymouth, to a Naval family, who shortly afterwards moved to Huddersfield, Yorkshire. Although I personally didn't live for very long in the North, I feel a direct familial connection with the Peak District and Pennines, having, at that time, paternal grandparents in Holmfirth, Yorkshire, and my maternal grandmother in Sheffield, Derbyshire. The outdoors always beckoned me, and perhaps this was in the blood, since my grandad was notorious for walking every day, for most of the day, over the Moors, myself and my sister occasionally going with him. My connection with Scotland is a stage removed, though feels equally strong, through the Macintosh bloodline on my mother's side.

By the time I was school age we had moved to the Midlands, first to the RAF base at Shawbury, and then to a few more rural villages. After the separation of my parents during my teens, we (my mother, sister, and self) gradually moved into more urban surroundings and more straightened circumstances. Educationally, I picked myself up from a disappointing start, studying a Science Foundation Course with the Open University to improve on my 'A' levels, and going on to obtain a BA (joint honours) in Philosophy and Psychology from the University of Reading.

During my twenties, after the beginning and ending of my first marriage, I had a suicidal breakdown, the culmination of many years of barely coping, and had the benefit of time out from university to undertake intensive therapy in a Therapeutic Community. I was married and divorced again during the time that it took me to see out my undergraduate phase of study, but in my thirties I finally progressed into psychology training and gained my doctorate in Psychotherapeutic and Counselling Psychology from the University of Guildford. It was an era in my life in which I started to feel greater autonomy, and used this to pursue my passion for mountain sports, leading me to meet my third, and lifelong, husband Andrew, and in 2005, have our daughter Katy. The pursuit of the mountains also led me, in 2003, to break my back in a climbing fall.

The largest part of my working life as a psychologist was as a senior lecturer and doctoral course director at Wolverhampton University, which I began in 2003. After a decade there I felt that the culture in education was changing and that I needed to leave in order to maintain my health. In 2013, with my husband and a few friends, our bushcraft and survival company 'Farafoot' saw the light of day, and since then we have both taken on eclectic occupations to support the limited income that it delivers.

Working outdoors has led me into learning about, and sharing, all kinds of traditional practices, from tanning hides to fermenting foods. It has also given me the time and inspiration to write, including a few short novels. I enjoy, and need, the freedom to be outdoors working on projects, and writing about the things that bother me and inspire me, despite the fact that I have needed to sacrifice material security to allow for living in this way. A year from ending my Expedition (spring 2018) will see us all moving to a Scottish Island, Gometra, just a stones-throw from Knoydart, to live 'off-grid'. This will present many challenges, including working out how to school our daughter, but is a move that feels like an important realisation of our values and interests.

Contents

Introduction

Expedition from the Backdoor: What and Why?

This book is about my 'Expedition from the Backdoor' – 'Expedition' because of the hardship involved, and 'from the Backdoor' because of the low-tech and accessible action of leaving from home on foot. It required thorough preparation, involved a journey into the (personally) unknown, and took time and tenacity to achieve: all 'expeditionary' qualities in my opinion.

The idea was to walk a thousand kilometres from my home in rural Shropshire[1] to Knoydart, on the West coast of Scotland[2]. I had no idea where I'd be sleeping, except that it would be in a bivouac. Uncertainty was part of the challenge, as was doing it alone, in fact self-reliance was an ambition that moulded my approach more and more tightly, so that by the time I'd walked half way I had stopped buying anything, had made my most essential items of kit, and was restricted to consuming only the food I carried or foraged.

The aim was to have an intense experience that questioned every aspect of me: that straddled the boundary between the personally

---

1   A tiny converted granary in Ditton Priors, on the side of Brown Clee Hill.
2   Knoydart holds a charm for me, and for many escapees from contemporary life. It is a rugged peninsula of mountains and bog/marsh-land with no driveable routes in to its main settlement, Inverie. You either take to the water or walk.

possible and impossible. Could I sleep rough, carry everything I needed and forage for the rest? Could I survive without modern foods and fuels, and with minimal kit? Could I manage my pain from arthritis and injury? Could I be alone and unsupported?

My initial motivation for the expedition was to validate the premise of my novel, INCH (I'm Never Coming Home), in which my protagonist survived such a walk, but by now that seems barely relevant. I suspect that it was my interest in testing the idea that led to the storyline, rather than the other way around.

The Writing Process

I wrote a diary from the start, and this has blossomed into a weighty blog, but only by posting 'retrospectively'. I wanted to restrict contact and communication as far as possible during the walk, otherwise my self-reliance would be destroyed.

What you'll find here are the raw words: the diary entries made each day; made alone but written into a context of my own expectations and my predictions of your interests, as a reader. You'll also find digressions into topics that relate to the expedition, providing the background and making sense of the diary. I've found that writing, just as much as doing the expedition itself, is a process of learning who I am. When I hear what I say, and see what I do, I'll know who I am[3]. So this book manifests my 'expeditionary' and literary aspirations and achievements.

When I read back what unselfconsciously flows out of me it is exposing, even when I've worked it hard and edited hard. I can't get past my own voice, my habits and my limitations. I would like to be able to write something that transcends me, but I'm learning to settle for trying to write honestly, thinking that writing *as me* is the

---

3   My adaptation of a quote attributed to E.M. Forster: "How do I know what I think until I see what I say?".

proper aim. But I must admit to feeling trapped with myself when I write.

Thus I've come to realise that I'm very egocentric, in a quiet way, and I wonder whether I can be objective enough to treat my subject matter fairly (myself, the places, the people, the experiences etc.), and with the penetration of truth that matters to a reader. Getting the balance right between my own perspective and someone else's (perhaps yours) is agonisingly hard, and I have many experiences of being brought up short, finding that I've misunderstood someone to my own benefit or at least to the disregard of their point of view. It's like having ones criminality discovered.

And that, it's worth supposing, is where my writing and my expeditions intersect; the fascination they hold. When I sleep outside I'm grappling with twin feelings: of **entitlement** (to just be, move, eat and sleep) and the **transgression** involved in being *there*, or anywhere. I've found, though, that it really does become simpler 'out there' because the choices feel compelling. Which is all very fascinating for me, and the project of me, but I want some of what I'm doing to be relevant, or interesting, to you too. When I think of the ways that it *could* be I realise that I'm probably not going to succeed. It would be nice to weave the diary of my expedition into the rich material of culture. I'd love to tell you about my expeditions with the authority and assurance of context so that you don't feel immersed in something that is unhinged. There's the travel and the places and the poetry of landscapes. They can't get anything approaching justice from my pen[4]. Neither does the historical landscape get any kind of portrayal. I know so little history that I'm a useless student let alone teacher.

I'd like to think, though, that I can offer an honest perspective

---

4   Henry David Thoreau in his book 'Walking', reassures me that wordlessness when it comes to nature is appropriate, and authentic: that we can't transplant our words to the page 'with earth adhering to their roots'. What needs to be understood is in the experience, the sensuous connection with nature, rather than in words and cultural knowledge.

on the rawness, the 'something-missingness' that is at least a part of some of us (I assume that it's not just me!), and hint at the remedies to this that I find in my Expedition. As with most phenomena, it is more eloquently expressed by a third party: 'Harmony, that was it! That was what came out of the silence—a gentle rhythm, the strain of a perfect chord, the music of the spheres, perhaps. It was enough to catch that rhythm, momentarily to be myself a part of it. In that instant I could feel no doubt of man's oneness with the universe. The conviction came that that rhythm was too orderly, too harmonious, too perfect to be a product of blind chance—that, therefore, there must be purpose in the whole and that man was part of that whole and not an accidental offshoot. It was a feeling that transcended reason; that went to the heart of man's despair and found it groundless. The universe was a cosmos, not a chaos; man was as rightfully a part of that cosmos as were the day and night.'[5]

About Me

When I was a very young thing, before I talked (whether I could or not I don't know, but it took me a long time to get round to it), I used to pack a bag, pick it up, and walk down the street. I don't remember this, but the anecdote seems to add some poetic closure to my story – coming full circle, after having departed from this strident beginning. 'Departed' in the sense that I was soon physically quite timid and unsure of myself, but fortunately that changed again when I was fourteen and took up karate. It was sensational to be able to feel each muscle work, and to be able to concentrate on one and contract it whenever I wanted to. It made me mentally stronger to have a connection with my body like that. The connection broke a few times as I physically matured and I struggled for many years with food: diets, fasts, binging, starving, purging – all the swings

---

5   From 'Alone: The Classic Polar Adventure' by Richard E. Byrd.

and roundabouts of disorder that are the norm for many teenage girls, and increasingly boys too. My relationships underwent as much flux as my body-image, and during my twenties I was married and divorced twice.

Notwithstanding these twenty-something crises, something drove me onwards. I loved throwing myself into things to see if I would sink or swim. Ever the experimenter, even with my life, I kept staying on the surface, and got myself a long way from where I started. They say your thirties is the best era, when your talents have matured, and I certainly felt that way. I'd become a doctor of psychology, director of a university training programme, and I was in good health and good shape. Mountaineering and rock climbing were becoming ever more important, and reaching 7,200m on Everest spurred me on to pursue Alpinism and high-altitude mountaineering. I met Andy, and, at the end of my thirties, had our daughter Katy. During that decade we climbed and we ran. Although I competed in races on the roads and fells, I always saw the races as training for the running rather than the other way around. This made me a sceptical competitor, but for a few years I enjoyed winning and took championship titles. Ultra-distance running took more precedence over the short/fast buzz, and I trained and competed at long distances over the hills. When Katy was small we used to push her round our running routes in her stroller (she dropped off to sleep as we left and woke on cue just as we arrived back at the house) and our neighbours still talk to us about seeing us running in all weathers with Katy.

I feel I can't leave out my big injury, because it has figured highly in every way. Back in 2003, two years before Katy was born, we went out climbing in LLanberis, Snowdonia. The 'Electric Mountain' is an extraordinary labyrinth of slate quarries, and I was leading a climb on a section called Holy Holy Wall (route: Zambezi), beside a grassy platform and round pool of water. The slate was tricky to climb and place protection, and when I fell, so did all my gear (my protection): after about 35ft

I hit the ground. The ambulance couldn't get through, so I was airlifted off, to Bangor Hospital. My body has always been reactive (Raynauds Disease, for example, cutting off the circulation), and for a while there were suspicions of internal bleeding since the readings were so 'off', but eventually I left the emergency room and lay prone and cathertered, with spinal fractures confirmed (later corroborated by MRI: crushed T12 and L1, with spinal encroachment). It was testament to the vigour of my family that I was taken from a geriatric ward in Bangor to the spinal unit in Oswestry, Shropshire. I joined a research programme into the use of braces rather than surgery, and within two weeks was mobile again.

Within another two weeks we were in Scotland, on the mountains. Mountain Rescue were out that day, perhaps searching for another casualty, and it made me awkwardly aware of the brace holding me together, and what might be said if I got into difficulty. It wasn't *hazard* so much as mental restoration that I was needing, but it was probably reckless from most other angles. I still have repercussions from the accident, but luckily the severe back pain is now rare. It has been superseded by hip pain and frequent immobility from osteoarthritis, which is an ongoing issue.

In 2013 I left the academic world, to which I felt less and less suited, and we started a bushcraft and survival company, 'Farafoot', meaning that now I have the opportunity to explore the outdoor things that inspire me, and to work on my writing. I give this as background to my 'Expedition from the Back Door', because although the expedition doesn't evoke the heights of fear I have felt on a rock face, or the level of risk of some climbs in the mountains, I count it as equally testing, and equally transcendent.

1

Getting a Handle

Art and Self Restraint

Richard Long made an artwork in 1967, which was called, and was in fact, 'A Line Made by Walking', by walking up and down a field, trampling the grass into a line. In a BBC radio series entitled 'Forest, Field and Sky: Art out of Nature' the presenter extended this idea by walking 10 miles across Exmoor in a dead straight line, plotted by drawing a line on a map. The presenter talks about having to fight the 'perennial human instinct to take the easier route… the trodden path'. He also muses on whether this can be classed as art – what aspect of the walk is the art?

This programme made me think about my expedition, and the artistry in it. I made aesthetic decisions all the time about the style of the travel, with an emphasis on making it harder rather than easier. I chose my constraints, and they were very personal to me: about being alone, sleeping out, being self-supporting, eating home-prepared 'traditional expedition' food, foraging and using minimal equipment. Those were the elements that made it 'artful' and mysterious. They were merely ideas, or ideals, but I bent over backwards to reach them, not really knowing why, except that the expedition would be more beautiful if I honoured its difficulty, taking no shortcuts.

Walking for symbolic, indeed aesthetic, purposes has a long tradition, and a lot of contemporary relevance judging by the number of people writing passionately about it. As my own expedition developed my conception of it also grew beyond materiality and into spirituality: I talk about it more and more as an odyssey. I've toyed with defining myself as, not only 'Solo Adventurer' but also 'Survival Artist' to try and suggest the more aesthetic side of this walk.

But it is also scientific in spirit, being a personal experiment to test my resilience in the face of myself and society. Thoreau, in his book 'Walking' comes closest as a philosophical and political antecedent when he describes the act of walking as activism, in defiance of a future (that has now come to pass!) in which people are confined to public roads, and in which walking freely 'shall be construed to mean trespassing on some gentleman's grounds' (p.17). Thoreau wished to experience the natural world in the least mediated manner, rather than through cultural organs like literature and sanctioned outdoor recreations. He sought the 'tan and callus of experience' (p.9), and so do I.

Camping by Stealth

When I talk to people about my expedition they tend to focus on the wild camping, by which I always mean sleeping out alone. The first question posed leads me straight into describing camping by stealth.

Q: 'Aren't you scared?'

A1. Well for me, a woman who grew up in semi-urban places, the biggest threat was other people. Out where there aren't so many people, they tend to get easier to spot and easier to relate to. The times I find my radar activated are near traffic and sometimes along easy walkways such as canal paths. Then I walk stealthily, let alone pitch carefully. Most of the time the people I've met have been more friendly than I expected, but once or twice I've found myself being stared down and purposefully intimidated. This happened twice in the Scottish Borders; once on the canal path and once in the forest, both times by lone men walking dogs on the trails in the evening. It had an immediate and chilling impact, and both times I had disturbed nights. My disturbance didn't manifest as worry over my safety so much as a diffuse bad feeling about the expedition and doubts about my ability to succeed. It was as though my energy had been robbed by those hostile faces and their 'bad vibes'.

A2. The next thing on the list is weather. For me wild camping implies being open to the sky: no tent. When I started out I went without shelter so as to be able to spot other people, but now I do it so as to be fully outside. Fearing the weather applies most when you are lost, or without ways of surviving being stranded. Which is not at all to say that bad weather is trivial. It's the element that often decides between what is possible and what is not, subjectively if not objectively. There's nothing more morale-sapping than being wet and cold, as I was in the Northern Pennines. My eyes were on the clouds all the time, even though I tried to accept that my vigilance made no difference to the weather. My fears were practical rather than mortal ones. Lightening is different – I do genuinely fear that.[6]

---

6 I've done some reading on safety precautions, and there are some significant differences when it comes to being out on the hills. The clearest one is 'don't be there'. With that in mind I installed a weather forecast website on my homepage giving detailed information for the hills. I had no call to use it though, since most of the time the weather conditions are fairly self-explanatory. I already feel pretty clear on the places to avoid in electrical storms, and the ones to seek. Its been hard to find consistency in the advice on emergency action, i.e. being caught out on the exposed tops. Given that in Scotland they are mostly covered in heather with enmeshed root systems and standing in waterlogged ground, then I assume that ground strike is as likely as strikes from above and that I should crouch on my rucksac, but I've even seen advice to throw away the pack and run (on the basis of making less contact with the ground). What is probably the case is that if I'm unlucky or foolish enough to still be exposed then it's all down to chance anyhow.

A3. Non-human life. Mosquitos and midges bother me badly. I can act like someone possessed when they have a go. And they did 'have a go' very early on in my expedition, during my first night out. My concern to be hidden put me right into the damp, dark places favoured by the parasites. The creepy crawlies in the grass don't worry me in the way they sometimes do when they are in the house (like slugs up the walls or spiders on the bed). I know that, apart from ticks, they aren't after me the way mozzies and midges are. The only mammals with sharp teeth that bother me are domestic dogs. Other than them, I can fear cattle and sometimes horses. But when it comes to it, usually they are confined. I don't *have* to get into the field with them. The open moor, however, is less controllable. I was pretty scared, as well as charmed, when I found myself surrounded by the eager faces of dozens of highland calves (very young ones) with no sign of any adult cows beyond the wall of their fluffy bodies. I had to try to be uninteresting and unalarming to them while I stalked back the way that I'd come, and circled widely back to regain the route beyond them.

A4. Non-human non-life. A lot of people are afraid of the dark, which I think amounts to fear of phantoms. Every person is susceptible to being spooked, so I can't rule it out, but I don't tend to have such terrors, and I haven't been bothered by them whilst sleeping outside alone. I've found that I'm more likely to be interested than fearful when I have unusual sights and sounds. In the Tees Valley, whilst lying down in the night, I had a feeling of something moving close to me and an impression of redness. These brought me wide awake and straining to fathom what was out there, but without fear. My imagination tends to tell me that it's a wild animal (once I've taken care to rule out the possibility that it's a domestic animal, since I do fear that – especially the human kind).

A5. Loneliness. I don't know where I stand on this one because if I felt lonely in my daily life at home I might not appreciate being alone outdoors. As it is, I love being on my own. I resent distractions. In the abstract the thought of being by myself can unnerve me, but on expedition there's been no call to think on that level. In the end you always have to get *yourself* out of emotional and physical difficulties, even if there's a rescuer beside you. I found that my mind has clever ways of buffering concerns about being on my own, and indeed boredom. I talked to myself initially, then found that there were other voices talking to me. All sounds became verbalisations, and some were external human voices. I also developed chants which played over and over in my head all day, but out of my conscious control. They even repeated on their continuous loop at night in my bivi. All these helped me to keep putting one foot in front of the other.

A6. Breaking the law. The transgressive feeling that might, in part, motivate my expeditions, can make me think that I'm being more radical, more anti-social, than I am. I think society suffers under an assumption, or maybe a wish, that the law is much more fearsome and wide-ranging than it is. I find it hard to hold on to the knowledge that just because there is no statutory right to wild camp in England does not mean there is an all-encompassing law to forbid it. And whilst there are risks of breaking civil laws, like trespass, doing so does not make you a criminal. I make it my personal law to act with care and respect, and I trust to that. I'm not saying that will necessarily protect me, because some laws are bad, or badly used.

A7. Getting lost. I take precautions: a map and compass. Then I simplify my mind with the thought that whatever happens I can always stop (before I step off a cliff in the fog for example). I fear going the wrong way and missing my route because of the awful hassle and waste of energy involved. But when you carry what you need on your back getting lost is less risky than it is when you are skipping from place to place without the means to stop. There *are* some objective dangers, like mineshafts, shooting ranges and military areas, that can make being lost more of a problem, and these have all made me feel more vulnerable. That's when you especially need a map, and/or good visibility.

A8. Getting sick. This one is quite nuanced. The expedition is in part motivated by pain and my mobility problems, so illness in that sense is inescapable. There are so many ways that incapacity can strike that it would be foolish to disregard the possibility, and yet futile to try and mitigate every chance. Calculated risk is the best I can do, and it does mean that sometimes I have real fears about my health, from anxieties about cardiac arrest to real incidents of poisoning. As Thoreau says, though, 'we require an infusion of hemlock, spruce or arbour vitae in our tea' ('Walking' p.26), by which he means that we need to partake of the wilderness, and I take it, by extension, the risks of the wild.

Preparing for Anything

My first walk – the inception of the Expedition from the Backdoor – was in September 2014, and added up to a mere forty miles. It took three days of the four that I had available, and I've come to see it as my trial for the Expedition. I was approaching fifty, the age threshold where it seems that every medical consultation is couched in terms of physical decline, making me more determined to push ahead with my Expedition.

My circumstances were similar to the other, later, legs: I was working weekends at the village Post Office and the rest of the week writing and working, along with Andy, for our bushcraft company. Katy was at primary school in the village. My pattern became to travel either in September or April, trying to avoid the insects, high temperatures, and numbers of people out in summer, and the unstable and inhospitable weather in winter.

Once I'd made it to the 'I can't go back on this' stage I was bothered and preoccupied with the uncertainties. They were built in to the plan, so it was a case of just leaving despite the queasy feeling: walking down the road and keeping on going. I'd read about Rosie Swale-Pope who jogged off, dragging her kit behind her, and kept going around the globe. She had wolves for company some nights. That's why I was so embarrassed by my disproportionate fears. By this age I've come to see myself as physically and emotionally courageous, yet the idea of sleeping rough gave it the lie. Sleeping out hasn't worried me when I've done it 'legit', so to speak, so I thought this fear must have been of being discovered by strangers. One of the most significant decisions I made was not to take a tent. On the one hand it chimes ethically – testing my self-sufficiency – but I can't lie that at this early stage it was mainly to allow for visibility. There's less fear when you can see around you, and on the other hand when there's reason to fear there's more chance of escape.

After mustering all the kit that I had (most of it over ten years old, and some much older), I managed to put together my pack. Throughout the expedition I aimed to use what I already had rather than buy anything new. My trusted old sleeping bag was 3-season down rather than synthetic, meaning moisture would spell problems, so I took a bivi bag in case of rain. Later in the expedition this combination failed me, leading me for the final leg to make a bivi bag that was less prone to condensation and to make a waterproof tarp.

My maps were also a hotch-potch of cut out sections (old cut-outs taped back together) of OS landranger and explorer sheets (1:50,000 & 1:25,000) and some printed screenshots, along with a compass (at this stage it was an attractive New Zealand compass, later replaced by my standard Silva one... for the Northern hemisphere!).

The aim to be self-reliant ruled out any use of the phone's GPS for navigation, or for tracking of my progress, and moreover ruled out use of my phone for contact with home. As the expedition progressed we devised a plan that I would message home every three or four days (signal permitting) to convey my whereabouts. Any more than that would risk the clarity of my expedition. In fact, in hindsight, I think frequent contact would have made the walk more difficult for me, since home would have beckoned when things got tough, and I might have resisted immersing myself in the difficulties of the journey.

For my rations I made pemmican. A related fascination of mine is the early expeditions to the poles and Himalayas, where pemmican was the staple diet, at least when everything palatable had gone! I took oatcakes and whisky too. I'm a romantic! I didn't take a stove, since I saw no reason to cook at this stage. For the later, longer, legs I began with a small gas stove then switched to natural tinder and a home-made wood burning stove (tin can with holes in it), as well as forgoing the oatcakes (not the whisky though!) and foraging for my food.

With each stage my dedication to self-reliance expanded in scope, until food, shelter and contact were all under careful control.

Pemmican: Discovering the Power of Fat

Pemmican has a long, and even a political, history (used as a pawn in the disputes over territory in the Hudson Bay region between the rival fur trading companies – Northwest Company and Hudson Bay Company – and the Metis (a mixed race people of Native American and Europeans) who produced the pemmican.[7]

When the land doesn't yield food, and you are on the move, you need to carry your supplies. If you pack a day sack with enough twenty first century food for a weekend away, let alone sufficient for weeks or months, you will either rely on dehydrated stuff or you'll need transport additional to your own legs. Dehydrating food is all very well, but demands that you carry, or can always source, fuel, and that the air and weather conditions are good enough to support a fire, and a hot one at that. At altitude, and in the wet and/or cold these demands are a problem. It also takes time and water in

---

7   The Pemmican Wars and Pemmican Proclamation of 1814.

abundance to prepare good food from dehydrated ingredients. So they are not as convenient as all that!

Pemmican has the advantage of packing so many calories into a small mass (a neutron star of a meal) that you can carry enough for a very long time indeed, and can eat it in raw or cooked states: like a lump of fatty corned beef, or as a meaty base to a cooked pot of starchy things. It is made from lean, dried, meat (think jerky or biltong) that has been powdered down or coarsely ground, and mixed with fat in a ratio of about fifty-fifty, with additives according to personal taste (berries, fruit zest, spices, herbs, cereals if you must… whatever). It also has the advantage of lasting for years, though the more things you add beyond the meat and fat the less time it stays good, measured in months and years rather than days. The power of pemmican is two sided: nutritional and long-lasting.

I had a quiet thought that maybe pemmican might support my smaller 'expeditions from the back door'. Wanting self-reliance, it was important that I made my own, though I've never come across any suppliers in the UK anyhow. The butcher advised that I'd needed kidney fat, since it is dense, dry and pure in comparison with other cuts. What's more I'd need a lot of it to get a useable return, once the air and membranes had been rendered from it. So Andy lumbered home with a heavy weight of the solid white matter and I unpeeled the bag from it on the kitchen table.

I was very white and hard. It didn't smell very much, and seemed easy to manage until I started to prise it apart. The lumps of fat were quite crumbly if I handled them carefully, but they were bound together in a sponge of membrane that made them difficult to break off. I tried cutting off pieces with a knife to speed things up, but the mess began to spread as the fat coated my hands and the knife slipped about. It wasn't like oil: you couldn't wipe it off things easily.

The pan was hot and ready, and began to crackle as the first lumps started to liquefy. I stood over it watching, trying to decide if it smelt bad or bland, and wasn't sure whether I could still see any of the membranes, or whether given time the whole lot would melt down. Being impatient to get it all in the pan and restore some order and cleanliness around me, I didn't wait too long before I was fishing out the yellowed lumps, rather than rendering them completely, and throwing them into a bowl to cool before binning. Several rounds of sieving and I had achieved a pot full of hot, transparent, yellow fat. I should have just rubbed the residual stuff left on my hands into my skin, but I didn't trust it. It took a while before I understood that this was the stuff I was made of too, and to learn that you can just as easily make handcream as dinner from it. At that time the idea of eating it was even worse than leaving it on my hands.

I expected the fat to set hard once it was off the hob, but even pouring it into a cold bowl didn't seem to have any impact. It took ages. In fact I don't know exactly how long because I went away and several hours later returned to a perfect block of white. There was no softness at all. I could push my finger onto it and it didn't give way or crumple, so it was easy to understand how it could be made into candles, as used to be done.

Now was the time to powder-down my pemmican ingredients: venison jerky that I'd made some time before and dehydrated fruit stew (of blackberries and damsons). The meat and fruit pieces were like little stones, though, and didn't powder down by hand, even with the big pestle, so I decided that in fact I wouldn't bother since it would be nice to have nuggets of lean food to chew on. But then, there would be huge expanses of pure fat to eat and surely that would just be revolting, so I added oats. I nearly missed the salt, pepper and orange zest, but was incredibly relieved not to have, once I finally tasted the pemmican. But first I had to make the block by pouring a freshly melted batch of tallow onto the dry ingredients and putting it in the fridge to set[8].

The slab of pemmican broke quite easily into bite-sized greyish

---

8   After the initial walk of 40 miles I was less concerned about the taste, and merely seasoned the meat and added the fat, leaving out the additions.

chunks, but initially I took just a few of the hard black shards of meat and fruit in my teeth to taste rather than bite into a chunk of fat. The flavours were really intense, and even with the coating of tallow in fact it was quite pleasant, helped a lot by the zest cutting through. So I tried a bigger lump. It was quite heavy – you'd never want much, but you'd not be much hungry on it.

It took a while to decide how to carry it in my pack, having had to deal with the mess left in the kitchen, from worry that everything would get covered in melted fat. But it dawned on me for the second time that this tallow was the kind of thing I was made of, and I certainly don't start to melt when it gets hot. So this fat wasn't going to start seeping out of bags or anything like that. I chose good strong containment though.

Respect to fat.

2

Expedition Part One: Trial Walk (The Initiation), September 2014

For my trial, or initiation, stage I was most concerned with whether it was going to possible for me to sleep rough: I didn't know in what way it might not, and that ignorance was my main focus and worry. Would there be hunters, outlaws, robbers and bandits at large in that other country called 'night'? Notwithstanding my experimentation with pemmican, the food was a lesser concern at this early phase, and had to wait it's turn for rigorous attention.

Diary Entry. September 2014

I went to bed early, and spent hours awake thinking that I wouldn't be in my bed the next night nor the next, in fact not until I'd found my way home from wherever I could reach in my four days. As usual the menopausal sweats appeared, and the hip pain was a nuisance. But my main concern was the morning. On the one hand my plan seemed to me to be ridiculously tame, and yet on the other it felt audacious. Was this any way, though, whatever the answer, for an adult, a middle aged one, to behave? Sleep finally came. Then it was morning and time to leave. It was mild (warm even) so I made some clothing adjustments. I'd probably sweat a great deal once I was walking with the pack, and it's almost impossible to get warm at night without dry layers on the skin.

Day 1. Ditton Priors to 'No Man's Green' between Alveley and Enville: Moonlight Bivi.

Left home at 9.15. The pack felt comfortable. Wanted to get past familiar ground and frustrated to be passing through known places all morning. Didn't begin to feel that I was really on my way until Chelmarsh. Difficult to use the footpaths since passed through farms with dogs, or signs destroyed/missing, or stiles rotten through. Not a good way to start – feeling like an unwanted intruder. Lost my way in Chelmarsh Coppice and had to bushwhack through. Amazing place though – steep sided valley. Enjoyed walk around the reservoir, then dunking feet in the water. Put sweaty socks on back of pack and felt at that point that the backpacking had properly begun. Hadn't anticipated using the Severn Way, but had to walk along the river because ferry shut and bridge private. Was checking all the way for bivi sites, and even escape routes – anxious practice.

At Highley – no fruits to collect anymore so got thirsty. Trees cut too high and verges clean. Pub in Highley shut on Monday – very Shropshire! Walked through Alveley (didn't like it. Bungalows on wide, fast roads). Very hot day so desperate for a drink stop. Went into pub on main road. Sat outside with beer and lime & soda. Insecure without pack on (felt too light) and back got cold even in the sun. As I got up to leave the bench, man who'd glared at me at the bar walked out through patio door and headed to his car. He sat in it, not leaving. Felt watched. Sat back down on the bench to wait for him to leave, trying to check what car looked like for future reference (habit!). After ten minutes he left, and after another five I did too, watching. It reminded me how as a youngster I'd walked at night, always ready to run.

Took road round to Birdsgreen, then paths to Astley then Filletts. Route finding tricky. Picked up bridleway. Dogs barking. Approached 'No Man's Green' around 6pm. Pushed through thick, low scrub. Found a spot with withies bent over and lots of leaf litter. Dragged stick through to find and cut away bramble tendrils. Didn't want to get all my kit out but came out in one supercompressed lump. Mosquitos homed-in big style once I settled. Already had on my midge net but couldn't see properly through it. Put on waterproof jacket and pulled wrist straps tight, then gloves over the top. Got lower body in bivi bag. Lay hoping darkness would send them away. Got really hot. Mosquitos got worse and worse. Constant whining. Couldn't re-arrange myself incase of making an opening. Realised I was in a swamp! Felt like tropical hell. Had to move on. When I moved they retreated a bit. Packed as quickly as I could. Needed head torch to get out but once away from the copse bright moonlight. Moved upwards to side of a field next to clumps of thistle. Lovely breeze – good night.

Day 2. Moonlight Bivi to a field north of M54 crossing: 'Oak Tree Bivi'.

Wet stuff in the morning, left out in the dew. Moon still shining during daybreak. One lost sock and lost sunglasses in the copse. Decided not to retrace steps though. Enville next stop, over rolling ridge (Sheepwalk). Landowner welcomes 'caring walkers' – funny. Large Hall, impressive grounds, and a tatty old orchard on the way out with gorgeous windfalls. Walled arena of some kind – vast walls. Jousting?! Change of scenery on the way to Highgate Country Park – large open fields, retention ponds, metal footpath gates and metal fences. Light aircraft above. Nightmare once at the park. Footpaths crisis-crossing and no clear Staffs Way path. Had to use compass. Lots of Himalayan Balsam. Too angry with the park to eat the blackberries.

After Highgate, scenery of golf courses (one at exit and one near Wrottesley Hall). Long Common/Abbotts Hill ridge traced the road so shame to have sound of cars. Nice damsons. Exit very suspect – had to turn sideways to avoid drive wall build out in way of the footpath. Lots of large houses. Horses. Ignored by a grumpy old man who nearly stepped into me from his garden gate – rather he sniffed and turned his back! Felt my life better than his. Found an iPhone on railway bridge and returned it to girl walking spaniels – making a point! Not finding water – getting thirsty. Found lovely ford near Pattingham – rather the road was a driveable stream bed.

Next golf course footpath squeezed through blackberry bushes and empty lager cans strewn. Easier to walk across the links but resisted. On the far side of Wrottesley Hall had to find the Staffs Way behind a small golf club house with private signs everywhere. Shock of fast road on the way to Oaken, then a kind of suburban parkland walk through hospital grounds to Codsall. To the pub! I was nervous of being trapped again. The last thing I wanted was to be inside (didn't want conversations and also very sweaty). Cumbersome going outside – pint in each hand (beer and lime & soda) and ski pole wedged under arm. Was irritated to be soon followed by a tall muscular bloke who took up a bench on the other side of the garden area. Soon, though, he was on the phone deep in conversation with his wife/girlfriend – clearly absorbed. Good. I could relax and enjoy my drinks. Found way out on private track – immediately felt safer. Long straight track over motorway. Looking for bivi and there were lots of good fields but too much traffic noise. Came out on busy road. Regretted decision. But Staffs Way took to fields again. Walked decent distance through dessicated crop and found grassy patch under oak tree. Perfect.

Sound of really heavy slow machinery on road made me worry about an evening/night harvest. Could see the top of it above the roadside hedge. Eventually threatening rumble went away. I looked at my maps and I knew that I wasn't going to get as far as I'd hoped. Slight sense of relief to not have to deal with Cannock Chase. The associations there aren't so good – something about the name. What exactly is a chase? Certainly looks large and imposing on the map, but not in the inviting way of the Peaks or Pennines – at least to my eye. Stafford sits next to it on the map, with a kind of sadness: a neither here nor there feeling. Ambiguity makes the whole area seem insecure. Maybe, maybe not.

Sound of footsteps and I was ready with 'sorry, this spot's taken.' A man's head peeped round the tree. A backpacker. Once I'd listened to how experienced he was at this kind of thing, pleased with myself to have settled on just the spot that he wanted. He noted the bivi bag, 'Doing it the hard way' in his view, and described the benefits of his Terra Nova competition tent. I didn't want to admit the real reason why that wouldn't appeal to me, especially after he remarked on it being unusual for a woman to backpack alone. He provided some interesting perspectives on walking in Scotland on account of the right to roam and the consequent lack of worn paths and designated routes.

Day 3. Oak Tree Bivi to Penkridge.

Walked together with David next day, more because he said it was nice to have someone to talk to for a change than my need of company. Nice man though. Good chats about occupations, that coloured the following chats about foraging, trapping, boots, tents, costs, and food. On Shropshire Union Canal I missed the exit for the Staffs Way. Really annoyed with myself. Abdicating responsibility for navigation? Shouldn't walk with anyone else again. Scene today was polytunnels, everywhere, and bussed-in workers. Lots of country road. Then BAM – Penkridge. Major road that impossible to cross except by diversion to traffic light crossing. David left to get provisions and have a cafe breakfast. I looked for the route out but confused by all the roads. Couldn't see which way to go. Sat by the road bridge over the river and felt insecure/disempowered after the navigation incident. Wondered whether to push on to Cannock Chase but decided to stop here. Headed for the railway station.

Postscript Diary Entry

I was out for three days, two nights. I think it was long enough to test the main components. I travelled forty miles, had two decent nights' sleep, and ate enough. The pemmican is palatable, just (but maybe hard for weeks at a time).

However, dehydration was a big issue, despite even using pubs. I need to sort that out before I carry on. My pee was really brown and there wasn't much of it, so I won't last long like that. I know a lot about hydration, from high altitude mountaineering and ultra-distance running, so you wouldn't expect me to neglect it. But each time I do something knew things come together differently. It was a combination of small things that led me to under-drink. One of the larger issues was the hard work of it, with the minuscule amounts I could get from my filter. I must get a different kind of filter that delivers more water more quickly, or I'm sure I'll be in for the same mistake. As for the other problems I had, the cause was doing things unthinkingly – by habit. You can't get by on cruise mode. And maybe it was taking things for granted that made me forget about electrolytes, and think that water alone would see me right. I had salt in my pemmican, but you don't eat much of that in a day. The irony is that I'd already experimented with sauerkraut as my electrolyte for long distance running, and used it a lot. The only down-side for my Expedition is the need then to carry liquid, but I think the advantages will mitigate the extra weight in refreshing and sustaining food.

Sauerkraut: Discovering the Power of Fermentation

The power of sauerkraut is, like pemmican, in its nutritional punch and its shelf-life. Fresh food is a necessity and a craving, especially when food sources are constrained, and when sauerkraut is unpasteurised it fulfils the brief. I don't count pasteurised food as fresh because all the live cultures have been eradicated.

The process of starting a batch of sauerkraut is simple: requiring only chopped/shredded cabbage, salt and a couple of weeks standing in an airtight container (but a proper croc will let it breathe so as to dispel the gasses produced, otherwise these need releasing every now and then). This was how I made my first batch, with added juniper berries for flavouring. The microbes on the cabbage leaves, and from the air, ferment the sugars, producing lactic acid. This makes the sauerkraut sour, and preserves it from decay. It also releases nutrients.

Sauerkraut has a much longer history than pemmican, used by the Romans and found widely in Eastern European cuisine, though also in Western Europe and America. Its benefits were recognised by James Cook, who used it to prevent scurvy on long sea voyages. Just the kind of recommendation I see as relevant to me!

3

Expedition Part Two:
'Sickness Leg', March 2015

Pre-Expedition Diary Entry, March 2015: Rampant Doubt

I'm preparing to leave and it has me in conflicts again. I'm still preoccupied with sleeping arrangements, leaving the daytimes to take care of themselves. My other overriding concern is with my physicality. I've been taking HRT for a few weeks now and for the last few days have felt floppy and uncoordinated – slow to think and do things, and sore all over. I'm not confident in my body at all. It became most obvious yesterday when we went climbing at Stanage, and I just felt incapable of anything. I can usually conjure up something that draws out the climber in me, but not yesterday.

Am I being defeated by my imagination? It might be that the burden of the walk is drawing all my energy away from anything else. I've often found that when I start the physical 'project' – the big run, big climb, whatever – energy comes coursing in, so I can do what seemed out of the question only days before. These past weeks I've gone for runs on alternate days, each time thinking to stimulate this phenomenon, but overcome by something or other (painful hip, lethargy, breathlessness etc.) so that I've felt bad from start to finish. And I'm puzzling over the possibilities: HRT, hay fever, poisoning, flu, morbid thoughts and other impediments, as explanations. But, and this is my hope, maybe it is my investment in the INCH project (my novel). It makes me stop short though because INCH stands for 'I'm never coming home', whereas I fully intend returning (the element of fiction that might come true?!). The walk was originally research for the novel, but now INCH has been written. And yet I'm holding on to the acronym that seems to make sense of what I'm doing. I find a great big lump of superstition right at my centre. But changing the name would knock me off course, even if I need to evade some questions in order to justify going.

I'm sticking to the primitive diet, even though I'm not really clear why. Self-sufficiency is a motivation from INCH and now I'm attached to it. I'm sort of trusting that the meaning or significance in this will come out later – on the journey maybe. It's like trusting the writer's muse and exploring something because it presents itself for examination. So there's a lot on top and under the surface. Why wouldn't I feel weak!? I notice that I'm taking a lot of products/treatments that are to do with my skin – the reddening and flushing of rosacea and the peri-menopause. Irrelevant, perhaps, outside – when exertion, windburn and sunburn normalise rugged, febrile skin.

Logbook: Written in the Raw

Monday 13th April, 2015. Penkridge to Bishton. Jungle Bivi.

The first day is over and I'm completely shattered. Andy dropped me at Penkridge, by the river bridge where I decided to stop the trial. I tried to fathom the route out, but in anxiety to actually get walking I just followed the road out towards Taddesley lock/boat yard. My pack was heavy but felt moveable, and I took on quite a good pace. Had a route finding issue at the motorway bridge and ended up on the Sabrina Way then doubled back. After the lock it was lovely walking through the arable land to Cannock Chase. Hot weather. Shugborough Hall alright, after ignominious ejection from the Chase along a busy road, then a long slog along the Staffordshire and Worcester Canal. More housing than I'd anticipated – very well to do, very tidy. Neatly fenced on the Shugborough side all the way along.

I was exhausted and looking for a way off to either side of the canal to a bivi spot, but absolutely nothing. Loads of people, on boats, bikes, foot, and road bridges and pubs to boot. Far too visible here. I began to hate boats and canals, and to realise that this was amenity land through and through. This more apparent when I decided to leave the waterway and strike out for farm land at the A51/A513 junction, Bishton, where the area was covered in brown visitor attraction/ AONB signs. Didn't look promising. Again, lots of large houses, horse fields and paddocks. Trudged along Colton Road desperately – hotspot on my heal, shoulder straps digging in, hip and quads hurting – watching out for potential. Saw thick shrubbery behind a high wall. A turn, small gate and jungly path. Squirrelled in behind a laurel, holly and yew – lots of greenery.

Now I can hear the busy road, see trains passing a few hundred metres on the other side of the playing field between us. Seems ideal. Basha is strung to make a barrier between myself and the house that I can just see through the scrub. I'm thinking after the first day that I need to get a feel for the scale of my maps – get my eye in. Also, I probably need to fill both water bottles before stopping. As it is I have no water for a morning drink. I'm wondering how this will go given having the sweats overnight last night in my bed. Well I'll see but presently so exhausted just want to lie down and relax. Not sure how my legs will be in the morning though. I've had a little nibble of everything and found that a small crumb of pemmican in my tea softens the flavour. Can't really drink tea without milk. Lots of midges (I think midges) around earlier coming off the water in clouds but don't seem to be biting yet – thank God! It's 7pm now and not yet dark but I'm ready to sleep. There's a rather strange smell that keeps waking me up though. Comfortable bed of dry leaf litter.

Tuesday 14th April. Bishton to Sedsall (Eaton Dovedale). Fallow Field Bivi.

Put in a lot of distance today, added to which some extra circles to find a bivi site. A mixture of awe and frustration today. Up at 5.30 and on the road by 6.30. I had a good night and seem to have recovered well (little sleep but very comfortable, apart from the smell. Watched the trains). Easy route-finding to the reservoir (main landmark of the day). No dogs about – I'm used to them out loose around Shropshire farms. Affluent area. Signs to stop the HS2 in Colton. Abbotts Bromley very friendly, and appears to have a few fields set aside for dog walking. The path out is through a housing estate onto fields.

Strong sun on my back walking towards Bagotts Park – an immense farm of immaculate rolling arable fields. Annoyed me that there was a dump of slurry, covered in flies, by a footpath post. Stopped to change socks and bathe feet in minuscule stream. Very sweaty. In a bad mood because of tampering/removal of signs from Radmore Wood and into Bagotts Park. After latter a change to sheep farming. Annoying. Lots of episodes of sheep trying to herd me, yell at me and variously stand up to me, also some farmers really obstructive.

All day the stiles have been really high (no doubt to stop dogs) so I could barely get over them with my tired legs and heavy pack. I've been refining my stile technique all day. At Scounslow green there was obvious obstruction, the exit from the field was completely closed-off with hawthorne and wire (tired and cursing I pushed through it despite injury) and at Knightsfield I was sent down a muddy overgrown gully, fenced off from the farm and drive alongside. There was strategic use of junk to make it difficult for me to stay on route. Relationships settled down on the approach to Uttoxeter, and the way was easy going. It was a strange exit from Uttoxeter from the railway, through an industrial estate, but in beautiful open fields very quickly.

Once on the main road I noticed a Derbyshire County sign. Thrill! The route from there was made easy to find although through convoluted, murky paths under the road bridges, with glimpses of dappled light and exciting water – the River Dove. Feeling very good. Doveridge exceptionally lovely, but very soon obscured in noise – tractor at speed in field below the slopes (I think), then clay pigeon shooting. Had seen a site for a bivi on the ridge, but concerned about the activity. Walked through the park of holiday cottages and shooting booths. Red flag up. Exhausted and just pushed on. Then bloody sheep and lambs as far as the eye could see. Thought I'd left them behind once past Eaton Dovedale, but more and more fields. No places to stop. Lots of planting of hawthorn in non-sheep areas. Took a steep hike upwards looking for cover. None really. Ended up walking out too far in Easterly direction but then I chanced upon a turned arable field. Somewhere to crash at last. House quite close and dog walkers went past on the other side of the field, but not approached. I had a spillage of unfiltered water today into my food bag. Tried to clean it up and didn't detect any actually on the food. Lots of sock changes required. Streams drying out already. I'm getting a rhythm of slow, even walking, telling myself to walk smoothly so as not to waste energy. Pack very heavy. Hot spot on heal not going away. No phone signal at all.

Wednesday 15th April. Sedsall (Eaton Dovedale) to Coldwall. Moss Bed Bivi.

PM. Another hot one! Went carefully for a shorter day today, stopping at the foot of Dovedale at 3.30 pm rather than pushing further. Then I climbed up the valley side to find a flat site. At first chose a semi-flat platform in the trees, half way up the bank. When I looked about it turned out to be between a fox nursery (prints, scat, lots of tracks) and feeding ground (bones, feathers etc.). Could have been a very noisy night. Also, the gradient looked okay from standing but I could imagine gently slipping and having dreams of the time I bivied with friend, Ian Ferguson, out climbing in the Alps, on the very steep side of the Ober Gabelhorn in a storm[9]. I pushed up to the very top and found a flat patch covered in dry worm casts, underneath a hawthorn tree. Collected dried up moss from the grass to use as mattress. Lots of signs of wildlife – dug patches, dens, tracks, piles of nut cases. Today saw a heron, a hare, and heard nightingales. It was tough physically and I took it slowly.

Have a deep blister now on my left heal, and shallower one on the right. Used whisky to clean skin and hypodermic needle to drain and micropore to push the skin down. Had trouble with hip as well today. Annoyingly today I did more miles than needed through walking with a meander in the river rather than cutting across. Thought I could see a prison ahead (or was I completely off course and it was Abbotsholm School?) It turned out to be JCB world headquarters in Rocester. Not so bad up close! Had breakfast under the bridge, where I picked herbs for later. Path through Rocester quite simple (a relief to me since I turn out to be useless at navigating in towns). Getting better with the maps, though. Very careful to get off the Staffs Way and pick up the Limestone Way. No particular trail symbol for the Limestone Way, just generic footpath signs (shame). Again, in Rocester, amenity dog-walking land on the edge of town. Change from ridiculously high stiles to some of them

---

9   In fact it was worse than it sounds. Lightening was flashing in arcs over the mountains, and I was surrounded by metal: crampons, ice screws, ice axes. Added to that, the slope was so steep, and so icy, that we stopped a sliding descent into the ice-field below only by pushing our feet onto a jutting-out rock. All that I could see when I looked down were my feet and the wide void beneath.

being the typical upright stones of the peaks and Pennines. Felt a thrill. Walked an idyllic stretch near Dovelays. Picked ransom and rolled up my trousers.

In Ellastone was disappointed with route destruction. Ended up stepping over electric wire to exit through a driveway because the stile had been destroyed. I guessed that I was supposed to go through the field of cows by the river, but there was no sign to say so. Became part of village life as sat on the wall towards the abbey to sort out socks. Nice chats. Hip went bad – very painful. Kept trying and trying. Thought I'd have to quit. Managed to walk through it eventually, having told a concerned man that once it was warmed back up would be alright (wasn't entirely convinced myself). Ended up at abbey rather than peeling off earlier. Lovely traversing path at Northwood, coming around the ridge above the trees. Picturesque. Stopped to dry gear (like a line of kites in the wind, tied to the fence) with views down to Mayfield. Treated to a good track towards Thorpe and lovely farm at Coldwall down to the river bridge. Funny, steep, undulating sheep field. Very tidy. River Dove gorgeous under stone bridge. An angler strode straight past me as I dangled feet in the water and filled the bottles, straight into the river and across to the other side, Labradors accompanying. Greeted each other. Stopped early to find my bivi on the river bank.

Thursday 16th April. Coldwall to Alstonefield. Tidy Camp

Morning entry

Not a great deal of sleep last night. Up at 5am deciding that I might as well try to go to the toilet since I'd had some indigestion and wind cramps during the night. The rain was only light during the night but it was horrid getting drops falling on my face so I'd crawled further down under the tarp and created condensation.

Then I had the problem as well of the poncho/tarp touching my face – damp and cold. In the early hours I propped it up with my ski pole. Need in future to stretch it out more and keep it away from my body.

There was a red sunset last night behind the trees on the opposite ridge. The sunrise was monochrome (thankfully!). During the evening yesterday watched dark mists growing and thought it mightn't be out the question to get thunder and lightening. Then what would I do? Stay put is what! Too much work to get here, and would be a big mess to leave now I thought! My body wasn't happy and I began to worry about my tight chest and breathlessness. Would I be found up here? But I resisted turning on the phone. Felt this way before – no big deal. But it got me thinking a lot about death and getting old. Maybe I didn't know when to stop and rest?! But having a bloody good time though! Reminds me of walks-in to climbs in the Alps, and climbing on Everest[10]. Incredibly hard work due to the weight of the pack that I can hardly lift, and yet I do it, and it works! In fact, the walk feels like high altitude at times. Bells started ringing around the valley off and on, and all the animals started calling as well – geese, sheep, song birds. Felt Alpine – the valley calling up to the pastures on the mountains. Made me muse on the meaning of the

---

10   In 2002 I joined a summiting expedition as far as the North Col (7200m). An unfortunate thing about Everest is that the summit fee (payable to the Chinese government) is so expensive that any expedition is going to cost more than I had, and am ever likely to have. So I went with a company called Jagged Globe through Tibet to the North side of Everest to join, for a short time, an expedition being led by Russell Brice (famous mountaineer who was, with Harry Taylor, the first to successfully climb the Pinnacles on the northeast ridge), and to go only was far as the North Col. I learned a lot there about managing myself at altitude: the ability to endure privation and to distinguish manageable pain and discomfort from signs of dangerous physiological changes. On an Alpinism course run by Jagged Globe I had the good fortune to be instructed by Roger Mears, a notable climber, mountaineer and antarctic explorer, who gave we newbies the benefit of his displeasure at our fumbling ineptitude, until we eventually had his pleasure at our efficiency. I learned from him to arrange my pack with the entire day in mind, and to stop rarely and briefly in the mountains.

church – how traditionally it holds us safe and gets us through this briefest life. Ritual, belonging, insignificance – giving us the power to continue.

Evening log entry

It looked as though today was going to be disastrous – several times. I was up at 5am, and after writing my log while things dried a bit, didn't get away till 7am. I set off slowly but was struggling a lot. It was quite cold and I didn't seem to be warming up under my own steam. As I walked up Dovedale I began feeling really sick and not able to breathe deeply. Just like being at altitude (a frequent allusion now). I had to force myself to eat and drink something[11]. Began wondering what would happen if I had a heart attack – absolutely nobody about. Surprised me. I'd have thought at least a few dog walkers. Anyhow, got a bit scared – alternating with not caring at all. Felt very light headed, and thought perhaps this, today, was my extreme 'vision quest' – bordering on hallucinating. The last few Kilometers in Dovedale went on forever. Tried to console myself that at least I wasn't rock climbing in this state – remembering the polished, slippery limestone. Noticed how slippery the rocks were on the path. When wet they'd be frictionless. Wondered why you never see fossils when rock climbing when they were everywhere on the path.

Came off at Millbank, where there was a DofE group – all girls, in good spirits. Began to feel better. Had decided to head up to Alstonefield to a campsite rather than push to get to Biggin. I desperately needed a campsite because not sure what might be going on with me health-wise. Wondered about the HRT and the new

---

11   There are many challenges to the body at altitude, at least before acclimatisation, which include loss of the senses of taste and smell and difficulty eating. If you want to stay healthy you have to disregard your queasiness and keep eating, just as you have to keep moving in spite of your altitude headache.

oestrogen patch I'd put on this morning, and taking progesterone even though I am now, unexpectedly, bleeding (too early, from stress?). Going to stick with the regime though. Wondered about sunstroke perhaps – maybe that was why struggling with my temperature – unlikely. Anyhow, tried to tell from the map which road/path might bring me out at a campsite. Followed the Sabrina Way up a very steep hillside and surprised myself that I had the energy. Sapped, though, on arrival. Not a soul about. No sign of any campsite. Wandered up and down looking.

This a very tidy place. All I saw were dustbin lorries plowing through the town, and various other amenity workers. One tractor. No other people except the backs of the heads of old folk in the community centre. I tried to get in to ask if they knew of any sites but the inner door was locked. A sign on the outer door said the post office was there, briefly, Monday and Thursday, but I was too early by far. Began to hate the place. Couldn't even find the pub.

Decided to trace a route to Biggin along Biggin Dale, cutting down to Wolfscote Dale to get there. The path should be opposite the pub, so I needed to find it. There was a school bus parked by a path and when I started looking at my map a woman jumped out to say the path was behind the bus (DofE). I chanced the question whether she knew of a campsite and she believed there was camping at the hostel further down the road. Found it. Hostel locked. Got talking with a friendly man doing the gardens. Private (pre-booking) hostel, he said. The keeper had gone to the doctors and would be back soon. I said I'd wait because I couldn't go any further anyway and that maybe he'd allow me to camp. He said that he was sure that Mr Teesdale, opposite, wouldn't mind me camping, but he'd also gone out for a bit and would be back soon. I followed him into Mr Teesdale's grounds. Sat on a bench. SO GLAD. £5.00 per night. Lovely, mown, camping field, toilet and wash-up area. I began to feel a whole lot less negative about tidiness. Apparently a chap stayed for two nights and left yesterday, from Cornwall doing the end-to-end.[12]

It was now 11.00am. I slept, washed, changed, experimented with stringing the tarp. Happy with the result. Went, not entirely reluctantly, to the pub (easy to find!). Incredibly friendly. Boot over-shoes (plastic covers) in the porch – well why not! – coats taken from my shoulders and hung up by one of the customers. What a (slightly insecure) joy to be without my pack. Blankets and cushions arranged neatly at every seat. Open fire, copper-coated bar, I wonder how I'd cope outside after this! I also wonder how my body would cope with rich steak pie. Treating myself to this in the interests of being able to carry on. Clearly I've been on starvation rations and doing too much work for the amount of food. Blood pressure issue? Very articulate people in the pub. Lots of banter. Most not local though I'd say – retired here from the city??

Friday 17th April. Alstonefield to Cheedale. Clifftop Bivi

Heading out from Alstonefield I felt rapturous – just loving it! An early morning angler on the river (mutual ignoring). Lovely valley scenes and stony climbs until reaching the Tissington Trail (disused railway and Pennine Bridleway). Another milestone. Pristine, bright, white underfoot (needed sunglasses even though cold, overcast weather). Had been sensing rain ever since campsite but none came. Quite breezy – North Easterly (cold) – so I had to keep adjusting from hot – cold – warm. Only changed socks once through the day at Street, so obviously much colder today. Cyclists and more cyclists. I felt like a pack-horse – slow, large, but also STRONG. Allowed myself a hot drink and teacake at Parsley Hay because from an

---

12   This was one of a few instances on the expedition where my path crossed with an end-to-ender (Land's End to John O'Groats). I always wondered what style they were using and how long they'd been out, and whether my own hardship was lesser, equal or greater than theirs.

outside booth so technically foraged on the trail!![13] Haven't needed to source water – foraged it also from taps on the trail! Good thing because I was worried when out of Dovedale and on the dry tops what I'd do for water. Spent a lot of time looking at the map and calculating distance/times, even though the route absolutely obvious. Signs and facilities everywhere. Fields are different now, past Street – small and with stone walls (many fallen in places). Not many stocked. Started thinking about a specific bivi site early, at 3.00pm, and found it at 4.00pm on a cliff top overlooking Chee Dale (Buxton water flowing!). Exposed but stunning. Strung basha against a wall at an angle to shelter from wind, otherwise would have been a wind tunnel. Very little pemmican left!

Saturday 18th April. Cheedale to Edale. Dysentery Camp.

Had a very comfortable night. Wakeful at times. Found the inside of the tarp got quite wet even though no rain. Must have been hill mist. Used ski pole again to prop up the tarp. Was visited a few times by a black and white cat/kitten, who nearly jumped out of his skin. Had a bell so I could hear him returning. Also, a farmer drove up and down several times on the other side of the wall. Not sure why, but so close he could have seen me if he looked over. My speculation was that the farmer on the other side of the valley, who could probably see me easily, had phoned him![14] I was too warm again I think, and I also needed a pee but couldn't be bothered to get up – doesn't help with sleep! Got up at 5.00am and struck camp. VERY cold wind until I descended to Chee Dale. Huge limestone cliffs either side. Steep RSPB path down – dodgier than I'd counted on. Then pulled out of the valley to Wormhill. Quarry signs

---

13 An indulgence that is anathema to me now, and has been since the third leg but there it is!

14 My paranoia was quite high on this leg of the expedition. Everything felt personal. Later this diminished as my ego quietened down.

everywhere warning of death. After the exposed tops of Wormhill
I opted for a low route through Monks Dale, Peters Dale and Hay
Dale (limestone Way). Extraordinary scenery.

Took local footpaths over trunk road (shock) to pick up
sharp climb onto tops above Castleton. All very quiet until Old
Moor, and especially the Rowter Farm track. Groups of older
folk heading over Ox Low and Bradwell Moor. 'DofE Central'
at the track. I dried out tarp and thermarest there whilst I had
a drink and some sauerkraut. A gate hanging on its side was
singing as the wind blew through it. Reminded me of Tibet.
All groups seemed to be talking of taking Mam Tor and the
benefits of. Shorts and teeshirts brigades started to turn up, and
I felt distinctly out of place (they're tough up North!). Lots of
day trippers (babies carried in slings) hauling up Castle Dale (a
stream bed of slick limestone blocks). Mountain bikers. Tried not
to let my expedition mentality slip. In Castleton, slunk behind
a parked car by the river and draped my gear over the bench to
dry in the sun. Quite hot. Decided on shorts now rather than
rolled-up trousers. I was debating whether to get water from the
stream or buy some. Lots of youngsters around the stream so I
did neither. Recalled that I needed cash. Must have something
to eat, but what? Also wanting a return call from home for one
I made as I walked in to the town. Hard to know what to do. A
town 'in the way'. Well in fact quite easy to describe – I hated it!
Guided groups, obligatory DofEs, school groups, tourist groups,
the rest rather boring holiday-makers. The place is just full of
Blue John gift shops, tea shops and B&Bs.[15]

Decided to get cash after drying sleeping bag. Weird experience.
Post Office closed and Londis shop it was in didn't seem to want
to give me cash back even if I paid. He directed me to a gift shop
with an ATM that might be okay (!!!). I couldn't find it. Tourist

---

15 I remembered as a child visiting the Blue John caves, and when I was older being
    taken into the potholes and caves of the Yorkshire Dales, and the fascination that I
    had; not for the stone but for the altered sensations of being underground (earthy

information directed me to one in a pub that turned out to be offline. Decided to walk away and towards the youth hostel. Found a deli and bought a pork pie, soft cheese, potted beef, seaweed crackers and pork scratchings (the potted beef and soft cheese were never touched. The rest, on and off, were sampled over the subsequent week). Got cash back for a £1.00 fee, which I didn't mind paying for once in my life! Decided as I walked to just strike out for Edale since the weather was so good. The cold wind had eased a bit and the sky clear blue and sunshine. Headed up Losehill. Tiring climb after such a long day (2.30pm by the time I left Castleton). Took some possibly dodgy water from stream. Staggered into Edale feeling ill. Rowdy bunch swearing in the pub 'garden' as a I went past. Kept head down. That made me feel more that I needed a campsite. Found nice one by the National Park centre. Set up in 'backpackers area' next to a large family sized tent! Suspicious looks from the blokes in tiny tents at the end of the field when I string the tarp.

Nausea set in and diarrhoea followed. Decided to try and get hot food in vain attempt to bring health back. Pizza from roadside oven (couldn't eat), half pint of beer at pub – not the rowdy one but the exceptionally good Nag's Head (apparently official start of the Pennine Way) – but had to leave it. Drank some lime and soda though (on the house!). Gutted, because I was starting to feel really strong. Started calculating how far I might get, but secret anxiety about transition onto the PW (Pennine Way). Odd. Some thoughts that I might have to stop, but I suspected that stopping would be because of the anxiety more than illness, so I decided I'd definitely continue once the runs had passed

---

smells, darkness and resonances). I've always been disappointed since with tourist caves where the lights and cordoned paths destroy the subterranean wildness.

Sunday 19th April. Day off

Morning entry

Had to get up three times urgently in the night and on the last two didn't make it! Had to wash my clothes this morning. Will need a day off. Slept well once nothing left inside! Hopefully careful treatment today should see me right.

Evening entry

No dioralyte! Typical! Nibbled crisps from pub, and sips of water. Had to take extreme care of myself all day. Slept. Made myself get up (more implementation of things learned at altitude) and take a slow stroll. Eyes and face hurt. Wondered whether this was going to be a migraine. Went to the phone by the Nags Head to call home but it took my money and didn't put me through. Man in local shop/ post office said, when I asked, that it was a known problem, that it gets used and abused a lot – vandalism. What he didn't say was that there was another box a short walk down the road! Beginning to worry about small post office owners. Extremely withholding![16]

Nibbled a banana all day, pulverising it before swallowing. Must get some food I can heat up I think. Tried to take some paracetamol and projectile vomited horizontally out from my sleeping bag. Thank goodness for the trowel! Otherwise all seemed to be well in the excretion department. Pee the correct colour. No unexpected substances. Tried to phone home again in the pouring rain from mobile (located a signal on the way to phone box #2). Really good to speak with Andy and Katy. She sounded good and hearty. She's a trooper! Been at our friends Helena and Mike's while Andy at work,

---

16 Being a Post-Office assistant myself, at that time in sole command of a small village office over the weekends, I have some sympathy with the deep frustration of the role, and perhaps the displacement of this onto the feckless public!

birdwatching, baking, drawing and playing piano. At her friend Finlay's party yesterday as well. SO PLEASED. So this afternoon, first test of heavy rain. Basha/poncho-tarp seems to be doing the job. Just a few adjustments needed. I'll see properly later. Looks like fair weather due to resume for rest of the week, though, so good time to be in the camp site whilst the rain is about. I hear that Bob (father-in-law) is offering to book accommodation for me from a distance. Smiling deeply! Won't be taking up the offer but good cosy feeling.

As I lay ostensibly sleeping a family passed by surveying the site for a pitch and dubbed me a "professional camper"! It made me smile, and also wonder whether it was possible to tell from the look of my pitch whether I was female. Was there anything about it that spoke of female or maleness? Curious question. Intrigued.

Monday 20th April. Edale to Crowden. Comfort Bivi

Evening entry

A tough day. I'm going to have to get used to the scale of the footprint map and not underestimate the distance/effort. It's quite sparse of information compared with the OS footpath maps, but then it's also small and light. Woke up with the Basha soaking and other bits of kit damp from all the rain. Decided to push on without drying it. Left 8am. Forced down some food before leaving (nasty expulsion of such at Upper Booth). Frustrating not to have the wider context on the map – can't orient myself to the landscape easily.

Some DofE groups (missed by leaders – they always seem to be chasing groups who've already passed). Felt okay. Took it, deliberately, really slowly. Nearly took route back South off Kinder Scout because misjudged the distance travelled. Orange peel trail over Kinder Scout. Mill Hill Post to Snake Pass a path of interminable flagstones. Couple of very concise conversations about my plans (Pennine Way focused enquiries). Kept putting off stopping, but eventually had a proper stop at Snake Pass. Clouds of insects (took me by surprise), but still not in biting mood. Dried out tarp and changed socks (4th time today). Very hot. Devils dyke dried out. Lovely mountain streams above though – idyllic. Started to feel hemmed-in on each side by walls of peat. Bleaklow like Dartmoor. Gritstone territory around Kinder and Bleaklow rather than limestone. Very sandy. Beautiful to walk on. But boulders on paths very tiring. North side went on and on. Exhausted.

At the river down towards the Crowden (Torside) reservoir I expected things to get easier. Not so. Unclear whether to cross the stream up to the 'Castle'. Did so over tenuous path and wondered whether to just settle in what was identified in a sign as the Pulpit. Pushed on and followed a narrow path, wondering whether this was correct. When Crowden came into view heart sank. Busy roads and long walk round. No thanks. Put pack down and looked for where to crash. Lovely dip with long grass, expansive views. Went in search of water. So near and yet down a very steep valley side. Dug trench for a trickle of water coming down through the grass instead. Sheep visited a few times but no other visitors except birds and insects. Starting to feel a bit more courage about 'winging it'. Had felt constrained by the PW, since it is laid out on my map from accommodation to accommodation. Know now easy to be flexible – should make it easier to look after myself. Will look for breakfast opportunity in the morning (and dioralyte). Party of three women passed under my bivi on footpath but well concealed

Tuesday 21st April. Crowden to Wessenden Moor. Hunted Bivi.

Morning entry

Woken this morning to glorious clear skies. Stars were abundant last night. Sunrise over hills. Frost on bivi bag and sound of red grouse. Had more health thoughts during the night and left eye hurt, but cared less! Katy emailed that she is missing me along with her other news. Emailed her back.

Evening entry

In Crowden, before setting off 'proper' bought foods from a Caravanning site – ones I thought my body might be happier to accept: jelly, custard (breakfast and lunch respectively) UHT milk for tea, a snickers for breakfast tomorrow and a small can of spaghetti for dinner. Quite a few folk out today on Black Peak, though still quiet and splendid. Stunning crags on the way up to Laddow Rocks. Also, lovely mountain streams again with beaches of stone. Changed socks about 8 times today since it was so hot, and exerting climbs as well.

Wessenden Moor quite different. An ominous place. Felt watched all through from the road along the ridge, down to reservoir where much work being done and men sitting smoking, with helicopter at work signs and taped-off paths. In bivi today at 5.00pm, again on my last legs completely and unable to go further. All day to-and-fro with the party of three women who must be the same who walked past yesterday. I guess they are B&B or something. Anyhow, at Wessenden I was starting to get annoyed with it, but it felt like such a god forsaken place, and quite a few lone blokes aimless down by the reservoir, that I was quite glad that they were behind me. On the way down the path to the reservoir I bent over to dip my hat in a stream so as to cool my head, and the weight of my pack pulled me over completely so that I was upside down and unable to get up.

Blazingly hot sky all day and completely clear – crazy. Nice breeze now on the moor. It may have been the helicopter spraying that made the place look so desolate and barren. It felt a frankly hostile place. Feel more rested now and beginning to like Wessenden.

Comfortable. The grass is tinder-dry so no lighting of stove for tea and spaghetti.[17]

Wednesday 22nd April. Wessenden Moor to Mankinholes YHA. Bricks and Mortar.

Morning entry

When settled last night had the works: mountain bikers in view, sound of road, military jets, airliners, then shooting began at dusk when I was hunkered down. Felt hunted. Grouse calling. Bad stomach again because I'd scrunched it up trying to get changed in a horizontal position. However – the good bit – FEEL HUNGRY. Frost overnight. Lots of dreams (one where a man gave me the security code to his house and was glad when I told him to be more careful). Red grouse everywhere, really going for it at dusk and dawn along with many other birds besides.

Evening entry

Long day again but easy walking. Kept getting impressions of Passage to India from the woozy sunshine. Hot and hazy with only the sound of my pacing and indistinct other sounds. Backpack 'speaks' to me all the time with little squeaks and sometimes seems like actual voices. Gets quite hallucinatory. Today felt ominous again in

---

17 I was now passing through the territory of my early childhood, when I lived in Huddersfield and my paternal grandparents lived in Holmfirth. Grandad used to walk in the uplands all day long and return only when it was time for dinner. I loved the vast bleakness of the moors even then, and was awed by the reservoirs that I was innocently sent by my grandma to play beside. But there was a sinister side that the moors was never redeemed from – the moors murderers – and as I walked through them I couldn't shake off the association. A whole landscape destroyed, as well as whole lives.

places – vast urban expanses pushing against the pieces of moorland I was on. Thrilled to be on the Eastmost edge of Lancashire on White Hill. Going over the M62 made me watchful. Truck stop on the road approaching the footbridge. Before that, on the hills over Oldham, bizarre scene: barren moorland with one after another lone man in knee-length shorts stalking about. Twitchers? Out of desperation drank some (filtered) water from one of the rivulets off the peat bogs. Flavour too strong. Drank my milk instead. APPETITE now good. Therapeutic binning of old food I'd been carrying and couldn't stomach. Had a small lunch at pub. Couldn't manage even half a pint of ale but managed mash and gravy and some pie. In the pub the group of women turned up again. I'd thought they might have decided against this section because not salubrious, but they say they are headed for Mankinholes tonight – the YHA hostel, then they'll try for Gargrave.

My next section of map (Calder Valley to Thornton in Craven) says 3,100 ft of ascent – SURELY A MISTAKE?! Today it was land of the reservoir again! I never found the direct route off the tops to Mankinholes and ended up walking up the road, and also ended up at the youth hostel looking for camping. Didn't intend to stay but so well treated by the warden that couldn't leave. Was only £10 tonight – maybe because the water was going to be unavailable from 8am tomorrow. Washed clothes, warden span them and put in drying room. Pub to finish charging phone. [18]

Thursday 23rd April. Mankinholes to Bare Hill. Rockpit Bivi

Evening entry

Had a good night in the hostel. Left early (7am) ahead of the

---

18 By this stage my self-reliance ethic had taken serious damage, and I was just getting by as I could. My physical and mental health was fragile, so I didn't eschew all comforts but tried to keep them modest.

'girls', and haven't seen them all day. In Bronte country now so seen signposts everywhere for all sorts (in Japanese as well as English). A lot of up-and-downing through valleys, but really nice scenery and interest. Seems as though this area, around Colden and Heptonstall, quite 'alternative' (relaxed folk). Really good day. Met a man with his dog at Colden Water who at first I was wary of (young, well built, tracky bottoms, tatts) but was really open and kind. He told me about May's shop and where to find it. Said he'd love to do this himself but not good with maps, and time scheduling doesn't allow. Asked me if I used GPS. May's shop excellent. Met a couple and they asked if they could try and pick up my pack because it looked so heavy. The man had a basha and his son was to buy him pint if he'd camp out under it. A lot of help in May's shop – cup of tea whilst I ate a yoghurt not yet paid for, gas hunted down for the stove (with citronella!), savoury rice in homage to the old days when I used it on my travels, noodles, banana, jelly babies (very unsure of the wisdom of that), dioralyte.

Route contouring round Heptonstall Moor missed, so I took the route over the trig point and back down. Frustrating that my map is limited – can't see the bigger picture. VERY quiet from Colden all the way to Pondon – then Bronte big time, although actually not that many people. Mesmeric walking on flagstones when tired – pack talking to me as well – over Withins Height and Top Withins. Nearly ended up in Haworth because got careless when hit the road. Doubled back in time. Kept walking to get out of the valley and find a bivi site. Was determined not to resort to a campsite – although didn't see one open anyhow – and wanted to be away from density of things. Just set up bivi. Seems good here. Two fighter jets gone over already and sounds of shotguns as well (but cover is good here in old quarry which seems important!). Clouds came in, worrying me a bit, so I messed about with the basha, but the clouds cleared. Cooked a meal of noodles on stove. Very digestible. Blessings! Birdsong and a rabbit tonight for company.

Friday 24th April. Bare Hill to Garsdale. Pheasant Bivi

Morning entry

Had another good night. No frost but cold wind. Quite exposed to wake up to! More cloud this morning. Expecting rain later today. Anxiously watching sky!

Evening entry

Not much time in shorts today – back to trousers after a few hours. Clouds, or rather hill mist, built up, and wind still cold, so without sun needed more clothes. Easy going over Ickornshaw Moor. Two Roe Deer approached when I was getting water at the stream – saw me but didn't run. Met a few hill runners today on Lumb Head Beck and Pinhaw Beacon. Friendly feeling – fewer hostile notices. Pub was not yet open in Ickornshaw, nor Lothersdale when I went through. Met farmer at Surgill Beck with two Labradors, one aged four and the other twelve. Shared stories of having a young and old Labrador. Kept me talking ages.

Route went awry and ended up in Earby. Hated at first because housing and yet more housing. Bought provisions at Coop. Very hard to get going again. Staggered along disused railway to Thornton in Craven. Route finding from Thornton horrible because description on my map misleading and also things seemed to have changed on the ground. Ended up going South on the Leeds and Liverpool Canal because of leaving Cam lane at the wrong time. Got my compass out after travelling a mile or so and turned about. I hate canal walking![19] Countryside after leaving the canal was all ups and downs. Tempted to search for campsite at Gargrave, and took directions for one, but put on a final push and got myself to the woods beyond. Stopped in

---

19   I have since discovered the reason for the route-finding problems I had on

a fenced off piece of coniferous woods – pheasant nursery by the look of it. Many other nice looking woods on rolling hills.

Saturday 25th April. Garsdale to Malham Tarn. Secret Bivi

Evening entry

Rain and rain overnight. Spent some time sorting myself out in the morning because still raining. Moved to more cover for a hot drink and rice pudding. Feeling okay. Planned a shorter day today – maybe Malham Tarn for a bivi, or the ruined wall at Tennant Gill. I found that my poncho wasn't as good as all that because it didn't cover my pack and myself as I'd intended. Instead I wore my gortex and wrapped up my pack in the poncho. That was alright. Proper Yorkshire rain today. I was soaking but warm enough, and happy. Went to the toilet for the first time in a few days now (no cramps or anything). Walked along river to Malham. Broad leaves coming out for the first time today. Lots of groups and individuals out for walks in Malham. More small children than in Edale.

Some cattle in fields now rather than all sheep. Clouds over the tops. Stopped for some soup and to dry at least my gortex jacket in the pub. Pushed on out towards the Cove. Only two climbers on the rock – bloody cold on the hands! Peregrine Falcon observatory going on. On the climb up the steps out of the cove rain started again. Covered pack with poncho, but fiddly with cold hands. Limestone pavement at the top wet and slippery. Lots of people there, badly dressed. Lots of groups coming down the steep gorge up out of the valley from the pavement. Out of the rain in my direction came the words "Dr Livingstone I presume"!

---

this leg. It was my antipodean compass, which was never meant to navigate the Northern hemisphere. The needle dips as it tries to find magnetic north through the earth because it isn't weighted properly to take account of the earth's curvature. It would thus get stuck, meaning so did I!

Once on the top Malham Tarn came to view. Picturesque. The large house turns out to be a field studies centre. Thought it empty at first but started seeing people all about – teachers! Couldn't find cover. Birdwatching hides everywhere, bat boxes, etc. it's all watching! And woods all deciduous, widely planted and not in leaf. Eventually climbed up behind a wall behind some houses. Set up basha against the wall. Lull in rain thank goodness.

Sunday 26th April. Malham Tarn to Old Ing Moor. Protection Bivi.

Evening entry

Dry during night but things didn't dry out. Company (mouse?) during night. Had to be very quiet because lots of chattering during the afternoon/evening. Up at 4.45am. Out at 6.00am. Very, very cold. Frost. Could only do small job at a time then had to warm hands. Steady climb out to Tennant Gill. Farmer asked me whether lost. Sun in my eyes all morning so couldn't see the route and slightly off. Was pointed in the right direction. Sunny day, cold wind – nice. Dried out my gear by the side of the road prior to the ascent of Pen-y-Ghent. Fantastic views. Many more people. Tough climb up the mountain and scramble at the top. Legs feeling the strain. Amused and impressed by woman in her sixties with standard poodle and grandchildren in tow, instructing the dog and them as she descended. Limestone – lovely formations from corrosion. Sink holes. Caves. Disappearing streams!

Had message from Andy that he thinks maybe I could get to Tan Hill Inn then need to stop. Looks good/do-able. Latest message, though, is snow and high winds with wind chill of minus 10 degrees on the tops for Monday evening onwards. Maybe I could try for it sooner. Intrigued about the weather – feel well equipped. Route not too arduous now I think. Had thought I might stop the expedition at Horton-in-Ribblesdale but keen now to carry on. Hikers Cafe – wonderful resource for Pennine Way and Yorkshire Three Peaks. Given their book to sign. Had bacon sarnie. Warned of bad weather to come. Patron didn't think there were any buses out from the Tan Inn if I stopped there and he would check, but I left before he had done so. Saw discarded ski poles and bits of ski poles in Horton bin! Three mile walk out to plantation at Langsthrodale for a bivi. Feel that cover would be helpful now that weather turning.

Monday 27th April. Old Ing Moor to Hawes YHA

Morning entry

Good soft bed of pine needles last night. In scrubby bit with some 'widow makers'. Very soft ground. Wind disturbing the tops of the forest, but not much movement on the ground. Bed early and slept. Middle of the night woke and began going through each day in my mind. When I got to 'here and now' it made me panic. Like vertigo. I was alright again when I started thinking of the route onwards. Very quiet in my little thicket. Just the sounds of pheasants and grouse. I stared at the basha and the camouflage pattern became like a Roscharch Test – I was deciphering the blobs of colours into pictures. Will maybe see if my sister can pick me up from the Tan Inn.

Evening entry

Noticed frost as walked out from the forest. Felt alright but on the walk along the high old Roman road I noticed a pain in my left leg above the knee (stabilisers?). Also had RSI in my right shoulder from using the ski pole. Swapped hands but it made me quite clumsy. Pains in leg getting sharper. Took it very slowly. Wonderful waterfalls on the way. Took more pictures (sensing the end of the expedition?). Maybe having a painful walk makes it easier to make the inevitable stop, so all the better.

Annoyed with PW paths in Gayle, on outskirts of Hawes. After long and painful descent from Dodd Fell (Tan End) didn't want to walk more than necessary. Disconcerted by Wensleydale creamery[20] but soon found the town. Had tea and muffin in a B&B and considered asking for a room. But knew I'd hate it.

Went to Dales info centre at the museum and uncharacteristically sought help with campsites and transport. Tried to find the campsite she suggested (very good help) but no joy. Just got to one at a fishery and got no answer from their bell. Happily set off for the youth hostel – leg feeling better. Didn't want to stop walking now! Got to the hostel at 2.30, knowing I'd have to wait till 4.00pm (turned out to be 5.00pm!). Who cares! Warm lobby with leaflets but feels like a school or NHS waiting area. Yet once the door opened so much help and a room to myself! Stayed in the hostel and ate my savoury rice.

Coach loads of students arrived & got drunk. Lying in my bunk unable to sleep but unbothered. Listening to the ferocious wind on the hills. Opened the window and turned off the radiator so as to enjoy it! Thinking about how I've managed my discomforts on the expedition. As in other scenarios I often think about the great explorers like Shackleton – well more his men left on Elephant Island – or soldiers on the front line. Puts a touch of dysentery and some physical strain into perspective! Now feeling very fit and strong. Heard of the quake in Nepal in email from Andy. Googled to find out more but found the news like pornography (press here for more pictures!) – disgusting. Don't want any news media in my life for a while longer

---

20   Made inevitable associations with Wallace and Gromit.

Things I will leave behind next time:

Silk glove liners (didn't dry quickly), Cap hat, Fewer wipes and tissues, Leatherman (very heavy and not needed), Dry shampoo, Finacea cream (skin treatment), Talc, Alum block, Insect repellant wipes, Hand warmers, Plastic ground sheet, Full length thermarest, Coffee powder

Things I will take next time:

Maybe tent and no bivi bag and poncho? (Inclement conditions), poncho but no bivi bag (hot conditions), A soft (noiseless) and camouflage-coloured ground sheet (maybe footprint sheet for my tent), Shorter thermarest / sleeping mat, a wood-gas burning stove rather than gas and pocket rocket, nylon liner sacks for pack rather than thick (noisy) plastic. Drinking chocolate powder, Salami, Katy's version of Mary Berry fruit cake, 60p BT payphone voucher!

Postscript

Diary entry from the Settle-Carlisle railway and Carlisle-Shrewsbury line.

Thinking about my walk in this early retrospect, the first few days were tremendously hard because I wasn't used yet to carrying the weight, and because the weather turned really hot, giving me blisters. Although the sun was intense the wind was also chilly, which was comfortable when I was moving, but I had to take care when I stopped, especially with my Raynauds issue.

The headwind was northerly, making the going harder but helping to keep the hair from my eyes! You wouldn't expect to get sunburn in the Peak District in April, but after a week I needed sunblock on my nose and on the backs of my legs.

The food worked well for the first few days, and I wasn't hungry at all. Most days I woke at around 5am when it was starting to get light, struck camp, walked for a few hours before stopping for breakfast, walked on till around 1pm before another refreshment stop, and then continued till about 5pm. I tended to be in my sleeping bag by about 6pm, had a sip or two of whisky, and made myself manage a few notes in my log book before my hands got too useless from cold. Throughout the day I took water as I found sources (clear, running) for my filter, and stopped to change socks hourly. But for the first few days, despite knowing that I should take them quite easy, I over-exerted myself, walking too long before breaks and walking too fast before my body had got used to carrying the weight.

In Dovedale I began really suffering, but after my diversion to the camp site and my meal, health was restored and I was ready to move on. It made me think about 'expedition lassitude' in the hilarious 'Rum Doodle' story, and their need for the delivery of cases of champagne. The result of that brief lapse was that I took a lot more care with my pace, deliberately slowing myself down even if I felt able to walk quickly, and trying to eat and drink more regularly. I still made the mistake, though, of not collecting enough water when it was available and repeatedly finding myself without enough overnight. I'd run out of everything apart from a little pemmican and a lot of whisky by the end of the first week.

I still don't know if it was over-exertion again or something foreign in my system, that gave me the runs and violent vomiting once in Edale. I needed the day off to sleep between toilet dashes. My trowel came in useful!

I also had time to read things randomly, and doing that I discovered that this is the 50th anniversary of the Pennine Way. I also read about the 'mass trespass' on Kinder Scout in the 1930s that led ultimately to the National Parks and the right to access the land. This seems to fit nicely with the ethos of my expedition since I was exercising the right to sleep when I couldn't move any further!

I became quite good at innovating ways to use the poncho, but the bivi bag wasn't a huge success. Even though it was 'breathable' the condensation build-up made my sleeping bag damp. On the clear, cold nights I wrapped up my pack and boots in the poncho to keep the frost off, and just scraped the ice from my bivi bag in the morning. It was better than making another layer of insulation that would have the ice thawing and getting everything wet. Striking camp could take a bit of time since I needed to keep re-warming my hands. On the few days and nights of rain the poncho worked well enough, strung at an angle and covering me and my pack. Luckily the sun and wind meant that I could dry my gear each day, but constant rain would have presented a more difficult situation.

My most difficult bivis were on the first night, through reaching exhaustion before I could be clear of a residential area, and my night at Malham tarn, where the only good cover was behind a wall close to a few houses. There was a lot of coming and going and so I had to hunker down quietly despite having walked through heavy rain and being soaked. Luckily that was the only really significant rain for the entire leg.

Passing to, through, and between the National Parks made for exciting transitions, and each time the geology changed, or the design of the stiles, I had the thrill of getting somewhere new. The livestock remained dependably sheep. I was surprised that there were so few dogs, working or otherwise. That is maybe just a seasonal thing – during lambing. I did see tell-tale poo bags left beside the trails – even on the Moors. Can't get my head around that – neither the need to bag it nor leave the plastic bag! What dogs I actually saw were all on leads. Around the attractions (like Pen-y-Ghent, Malham Cove, Cow Low by Castleton, Kinder Scout, the Howarth area, etc.) there were people about, many from overseas, but outside of those places people were rare – mostly the occasional cyclist. Later in the season is probably busier.

Travelling in April is quite magical since its nesting time. The cover is limited though, the leaves not being out, and it was surprising how few coniferous woods I found. One enduring sound I have is of Red grouse. The other is of my pack gently squeaking, accompanied by my pole tapping. Walking alone looking down at the flagstones on some of the trail tended to put me in trances. It made me consider that my expedition was spiritual as much as it was anything else – like a pilgrimage or vision quest. The heat of the sun intensified the smells and created the kind of woozy feeling that you get in the desert or on a sultry beach. It reminded me of the walk to the caves in 'A Passage to India'. My bivi on Wessenden Moor gave me a different kind of twist in perception: feeling hunted, like the Red grouse who were calling over the entire moor. I didn't want too much involvement with anyone, so I was pleased that the few chats I had lifted my spirits rather than annoyed or oppressed me.

My stay at the hostel in Mankinholes was actually unintentional, but very welcome. The day had been a long one and I couldn't find a good site to stop, so I wanted a camp site. Rehearsing questions about whether they would allow camping in the hostel grounds, I stood and waited in the lobby. When the warden came in she exclaimed, before I'd said anything, that she'd get me sorted – a 'wait there while I go around' and off she sped. When she opened the glass window she had all the paperwork ready and said that although I wasn't pre-booked she couldn't possibly turn me away. I wonder what I must have looked like! It was a lovely experience and I had a good night.

Every few days I emailed home. Characteristically, Andy was more than happy to do the work while I continued. Katy sent me regular messages, so I switched the phone on to test the signal each night or morning, giving me a chance to take a few pictures as well. I was very determined to use the phone as little as possible, not just to conserve power but also to protect the clarity of my expedition.

After fourteen days of, mostly, unseasonably good weather, I was being informed everywhere I went that it was all about to change and that snow and strong winds were expected on the tops. I needed to get home for work within three more days, and possible routes out were getting thin in terms of public transport. But I was feeling strong and toyed over and over with pushing on further. I had winter clothes with me (barely worn till now), mountaineering mittens, sleeping bag liner and plenty of gas for the stove, so I thought I'd be able to survive winter conditions. However, I might miss my deadline out. My leg injury helped me to be philosophical about stopping.

In the youth hostel, not sleeping, I rehearsed the past few weeks, trying to recall the sequence of the journey, and was struck by how lucky I'd been, with the big things like the weather, but also the small details, like: finding windows of sun and wind at just the right time to get everything dry, spotting water when I'd just run out, chancing upon shelter from the wind when it had begun to really hurt, getting rooms at Mankinholes and Hawes Youth Hostels, being given help to find camping from the gardener at Alstonefield, being told about May's shop, and even straining my knee to make me stop ahead of the snow. I hope that this will help me trust the process more next time, and not work myself up ahead of leaving.

4

Expedition Part Three:
'Bad Weather Leg', September 2016

During this stage I suffered the worst weather of the expedition, so I've come to see it as my 'bad weather' leg. It led me to think carefully about my kit and make a few radical purchases in anticipation of even harder conditions on Part Four.

Pre-Expedition Diary entry, June 2016: My Gap Year

It's been over a year since my expedition paused at Hawes, and it's been frustrating to see the spring come and go and not to have completed the rest – to Knoydart. Although finding the spare time has been an issue, it's been not half the problem compared to injury. In fact, since October last year (2015), only six months after I made it to Hawes, I've been incapacitated with arthritis in my right hip. It's been a palaver of guesswork and waiting to get to a point where the diagnosis makes sense to me (diagnosis being: moderate to severe osteoarthritis in the right hip, with dysplasia and inflammation). The hip is, it seems, too far gone for any remedial kinds of surgery to the cartilage.

I was hill running quite well last summer, after the second leg of the expedition, then around October time I had a bout of pain in my right hip, knee and leg and couldn't hobble far at all. Over the years these kinds of flare-ups have come and gone, and I've tended to think it must be something systemic since my entire body was always a wreck for a while until whatever it was subsided. The difference this time was that the pain wasn't going away and that my knee was also bad, making moving around even more of a problem than when it was just the hip. To put it in context, I've been used to aches and pains of the back and hips, which have sporadically affected for me for over a decade since my rock-climbing accident in 2003, so the hip issue has coincided with other pains and gone undiagnosed. In November I saw my G.P. and asked for a referral to a sports injury clinic. They diagnosed osteoarthritis and dysplasia, but not in a manner that I could easily take on board. Given that I've suffered flare-ups since my thirties it was difficult to accept that it was purely degeneration – an ageing process. I've now seen a consultant privately (funded by my exceptionally generous father-in-law). I've been talked-through my scans, and the damage is obvious. Most importantly for me though, my own reading-around has indicated that dysplasia can cause osteoarthritis in younger people, meaning to me that I'm a normal mid-life adult with some explicable damage. After some very depressing months I feel able once again to view myself as having physical potential to tap, rather than as someone who needs to take it easy. This, in spite of the fact that I am (still) going through my menopause, and have those sadly-named 'degenerative changes' to my hip.

This middle-aged era is paradoxical, and sends me a bit mad. I'm not in line for a hip replacement because I'm too young for that (although I've heard of plenty of younger people who have had joints replaced), but for eight months I've been less able to get around than most of the seventy and eighty year-olds that I know.

The booklet given to me by my G.P. sets out the latest non-surgical recommendations, but speaks to a version of me that I expect to reach in 20 or so years. It refers the reader to Age-UK, for instance, when I won't be at the current retiring age for another 15 years.

Diagnosis confirmed, I'm onto the treatment side of things now. Last week I had a steroid injection into the hip, which seems to be relieving the pain so long as I stay sedentary. Again, walking sets it off. One very interesting comment from the consultant was that all the damage has been done already, so I should do whatever I want to without worries about making it worse.

In January I joined a gym, which has rescued me from the depression that set-in around December (particularly poignant when I couldn't bring myself to un-box my presents from Andy and Katy of lightweight gear for my expedition). The revelation that cheered me up was the discovery that I could cycle on the static bikes without pain. With the increase in my physical confidence I tried to go out running, but both times I ended up in agony. So I've had to stick with cycling and weights (not much walking, even around the shops, and no remote chance of running). I'm fit as a flea and desperate to move, but stuck in a gym (albeit a really nice one with watt-bikes) or in and around the house, rattling with pills (mainly replacement hormones and pain killers).

I keep thinking about an elderly lady called Iris (mother of our friends, Mike and Helena) who I was helping to look after during last summer. She was hating being stuck in the house on a chair and kept saying 'don't get old', telling me to live while I could. It seemed quite morbid at the time, and I just wanted to get away from that particular conversation, but now I'm obsessed with the idea. I'm worried that by the time I qualify for a hip replacement, and go through the rehab process, I won't be able to make good use of it, and by extension I certainly won't be able EVER to complete my expedition. That statement is not acceptable to me. I'm going in the spring of 2017, or possibly sooner given the strength of my feelings, and that is that. I'm not growing old gracefully am I? But

I'd like to point out that there's no reason why I shouldn't do other things gracefully.

Blog Entry, August 5th 2016: 'Back Out There'

How far can I get in nine days, in September? That's what I have. Its not long, but it's all mine. September's a good month for weather… usually. It's not so good for insects, and it's hunting season for game, so I might need to watch my sanity. The foraging is excellent, though, so my morale might get a lift.

In truth I'd go regardless, since otherwise I can't get on the trail till spring. Given how I'm feeling currently I think I might be able to finish the Pennine Way, 'all being well, and the creeks don't rise', which will prepare me nicely for a longer stint to complete the route (from the end of the PW to Knoydart) at Easter-time next year.

Having to do this in small bites is disappointing, and makes distances covered per day more important than they should be. To make the best of this enforced brevity my plan for the nine days is to manage entirely on my primitive diet of home-made pemmican and sauerkraut (apart from water, whisky and foraged herbs/roots/fruits/nuts, that is). I might also restrict myself to a home-made wood-gas burning stove (made from tin cans) for heating water. Its a shame not to use the modern gas-fired Tilley lamp that I had for Christmas, but it'd be excessive to take gas as well. I'll probably use gas on the longer (colder) leg through Scotland at Easter, depending upon how it goes with the tin-can stove.

I seem to have acquired a bit of a reputation locally for accidents and incidents. I think it has more to do with what I've been up to, though, than any abnormally bad luck. There were the sheep, geese and dog troubles earlier this summer, when I was minding a small-holding (one sheep died and I had to deal with that, one goose that was determinedly nesting disappeared for good, and the rather jumpy dogs pulled me over face-first along the gravel), and since then, in the past week in fact, I've had an allergic reaction to a wasp sting to my thumb, which adds a more relevant complication to my expedition. Additional to the rashes, cramps, and puking only my ears and face swelled up, but next time it could be worse. I suppose I need to ask for an Epipen (adrenaline self-injector), but I'm getting a bit tired of bothering the doctor. I didn't need any adrenaline for the sting last week, only steroids, and I'm not admitting to being ill-feted, but when I'm out on the hills adrenaline might sometimes be in short supply.

Diary entry, August 27th 2016: Mortality

Feeling subdued – mortality?

Blog Entry. Thursday 1st September 2016: Countdown Begins

Tomorrow I'm off: 5.30am from Shrewsbury by train via Crewe, Leeds and Garsdale, then a bus to Hawes to pick up the trail where I left off. There's 151 miles of the Pennine Way remaining. I just hope that my head settles down a bit because I've been clumsy and forgetful all week.

A few weeks ago I was quite flat (not depressed but withdrawn I'd say) which has been replaced with this fly-in-a-bottle craziness. One of my 'special thoughts' was brewing and maybe it was *that* getting me down. It isn't the kind of thinking you can talk about, but maybe I can write it out: it's about mortality again, but with more a feeling of puzzlement rather than panic, sadness or anything else. I've grown to feel more and more connected with nature, and so it's hard to imagine myself being 'kicked out' at some point. It's not so much existential anxiety as existential confusion. It makes me think that I need this walk for spiritual reasons, and if the last walk was anything to go by the mortality question will get into my head again out there.

I've been juggling lists all week and I think I'm pretty much set with the kit.

Pemmican Changes and Sauerkraut Disasters

Yesterday there was a bit of a last minute change of plan on the sauerkraut. Such a shame. I opened up the pot and the smell was really odd: not the normal tangy pungency but sweeter and a bit 'off'. There was a white film over the top and no bubbles of gas coming through. It looked quite dead really. From what I can gather it was probably a yeasty growth. Like many of the moulds it's safe to just skim it off the top, but the yeasty taste and smell is off-putting. I took a small bite and Andy took a spoonful and we waited. By the end of the day we were both queasy so that was that. With it being a third of my diet it might not be a good thing to rely on it. I thought it was too late to replace it but my sister's managed to get some unpasteurised sauerkraut (being delivered today). I've made my pemmican using fat from other cuts of beef rather than kidney fat, since it is probably going to be easier to palate, and I've decided to take some semi-dried fruit that I've pulverised with a rolling pin to get it into a beaker.

My bivi bag was in a state because the seam tape was all falling off so I bought some iron-on tape to re-do it. Turned out, though, that the old tape stuck back down with the hot iron, so I haven't needed the new roll. I'm taking two poles incase of hip failure, but rather than buy a new one I'm taking a chance on two that I've made (one from Hazel, and the other from Ash). The ash stick is quite exotic, with a curvy fork at the top (trident!). To protect them from wear-and-tear I've covered the ends in rawhide[21]. No more tap-tapping!

After packing it all during my lunch break today it weighed-in

---

21   This was a mistake since wet rawhide is quite a slippery material!

at 15 kilos, which is two kilos lighter than the pack on the previous leg of the expedition.

For kit list and food rations please see appendices.

Logbook: Written in the Raw

Friday 2nd Sept 2016. Hawes to Thwaite. 'First Night' Bivi

Friday pm

Reached Hawes just before 11.00am and bought my Whisky. No skimping, got some Jura. Set out over Great Shunner (great name!). Uncoordinated with poles and fumbling about at stiles trying to get through spaces too small for pack. No technique yet. Straps digging in shoulders. A bit of a mess.

Once climbing up the track got into more of a rhythm. Tasted my pemmican for first time on top of the hill. Good job I liked it. Sort of everlasting corned beef – it chews for a very long time. Sauerkraut okay but not as good as my own would be. On top wind and rain came in. Very wet feet. Sock change on top. Really quiet but eventually heard my first red grouse. Seem much more reticent to call than in spring – who can blame them! Black rabbit dashed out in front of me on haul to summit – could omen? Who knows? Coming off the top saw Thwait in pool of sunlight – Meadowy dish in the valley. Gorgeous. Big contrast with Great Shunner looking blackly. In fact clouds building up and gusts of wind. Having two poles means can't hold map – bit awkward. Made myself eat and drink.

Did 10 miles today and completely shattered. Feeling guilty because tried to message Andy and Katy just now, once set up bivi, and no signal (could have told him I'd arrived safely at Hawes but too keen to get going).

Sky clearing a bit now (1830) and getting colder. Making myself write log with cold fingers.

Journey on train this morning really good/easy but felt self-conscious about my poles. The longer one looks like some sort of totem, and I was treated a bit like a (potentially) crazy woman. When reached Garsdale nobody blinked though.

Bivi tonight is just above farmland in meadow – just in the 'rough' behind a dry stone wall. Dogs barking – think they know I'm here, but then they probably bark at everything. Valiantly avoided using the wall to string out tarp (doing no damage – no dislodging of stones). Bent tree branches over top instead, but not sure the setup will keep out the rain. Not using bivi bag – at least will start out that way.

Very sore neck – a lot of pressure from pack on downhills. Patches of long red grass on Great Shunner looked like pools of shimmering blood – in a nice way! Lots of flagstones over marshy ground, many had bolts sticking up out of them. Not so good if careless or in dark. Had to be really careful. Got a bit strange after 3 hours out on the fell. Maybe not enough food/drink. Maybe shock of exertion. Better now. Eaten well on my ration.

Took from 1100 to 1730 to do 10 miles. Maybe will be okay pace to finish. Maybe even doing that I'll get too exhausted. Feet sore but no blisters. Continually talked to myself all day, especially pm when started to hurt. Told self that it is just pain in the hip and knee and not signifying any damage being done. Pacing is key I think. Hope I haven't overdone first day.

Saturday 3rd Sept. Thwaite to God's Bridge nr Bowes. 'God's Bridge Bivi.'

Saturday am

Up at 5.30. Still darkish. Quite cramped. Took inflated sleeping mat out of sleeping bag eventually since with it no room at all and v.v. uncomfortable. Supposed to use it inside bag to protect it, but little room in a mummy bag to begin with. Was alternating hot and cold all night. No good. Dinner was cold pemmican, but all nourishing. Breakfast: dates and sauerkraut. Plenty to drink. Aching a lot. Threats of rain all night but nothing much. Red sky at dawn though…

Experimenting with charger for phone. No clue how may charges I'll get from it, so will keep topping up so don't end up too low.

Saturday pm

Left Thwaite at 7am. Straight into climb over Kisdon. Mist. River in valley. Warm. Groups of red grouse looking picturesque on the boulder fields. Took detour into Keld to try and phone home. Rubbish public phone wouldn't connect me. Very slippery on path which problem with heavy pack. Lovely waterfall where considered getting stove out for a drink, but too concerned to get mileage.

Higher ground soon then lovely long easy up the Stonesdale valley. Rain came first as mist. Quite refreshing. Didn't cover up. Enjoyed drizzle keeping me cool. But soon came heavier and by then felt no point getting out goretex. Wrong. Winds whipped rain across Stonesdale moor which went on for ever. Just holding out for Tan Hill Inn (Highest pub at 1785'). When got there all I wanted was a shelter to sort myself out, but nothing. Determined not to go in. Have to be unsupported. Used outside loo to change into dry gear and waterproofs. Phone signal at last. Flurry of beeps and messages but just want say okay. Set out over the moor alongside Frumming Beck. Felt very intrepid setting out in that. Soaked at once. Very deep marsh. Water well above boots. Feet sliding around inside socks. Went half a mile and doubled back. Took the alternative route along road then track. Miserable situation. Worried how I could sleep out and where. Bleak – no cover.

My old map shows a natural rock bridge over Sleightholm Beck, but just pile of rocks now. Annoying back-and-forth to find bridge over beck.

Rain briefly stopped after Bowes Fell but began again. On valley side could see below clump of conifers off to west. Would try for that. After crossing dry riverbed!! (In this rain!) before climb up to cross the A66 I saw old/disused railway remnants (bridge pedestals etc). Found a stone archway which was completely dry underneath. Managed to change standing upright (luxury) and take my time reorganising my things, hanging some up to 'dry'.

Heard water but now can pay attention to surroundings more. Am opposite a natural limestone bridge called 'Gods Bridge'. Can hear the water moving through the little cave underneath the overhanging blocks on the tops of the riverbank.

Beginning to get cold. Think I'll try a fire for a drink. Looks as though weather due to improve Tuesday. Hope I can make it till then.

Sunday 4th Sept. God's Bridge to Tees Valley nr Middleton-in-Teesdale. 11m. 'Hazel Tree Bivi.'

Left Gods bridge at 8am. Had a good nights sleep. Woke at 7am. Initially could hear music from house behind me but soon went quiet. Water began dripping through ferns on ceiling during night, but managed to stay out of it. Clothes from yesterday all still soaked. Even bumbag and pack sodden. Foolish. Should have covered all in poncho. Must be much heavier now. But feel saved from disaster by my cave.

Struck out for A66 underpass onto Bowes moor. Very marshy. (Wore gaiters, goretex jacket and waterproof trousers over long johns, but gaiters not much use in bog like this. Beginning to think would be better to have boots with holes to let water run through.) threatened rain all the time and occasional showers over moors. Around Lunedale (Grassholm reservoir) all farmland and lack of signage. Got trapped in fields. Found a way out through field with bull, cows and calves – not ideal. On top of Harter Fell became easy at last and nice going underfoot. Went into Middleton-in-Teesdale and nothing helpful there. Wanted a nice stone bus shelter or something for respite, and a gear shop for some dry (hopefully sealskin) socks. Remembered it was Sunday – took wind out of my sails. Ended up in a plastic open bus shelter with sloping seats (like in cities). Bought two pairs of ordinary high wool content socks from the post office/store.

Saw some ominous clouds to North on my way over Harter Fell and wanted fiercely to keep myself dry now that my pack, bumbag and clothes had dried out. Only very light rain came through. I continued along Teesdale. Beautiful.

4pm. Found myself a friendly hazel tree. Sheep sorrel everywhere and lush grass. No thistles. Walked about barefoot to try and bring feet back to life. It worked. Have time in evening sun to hang things on trees to dry and have the perfect bivi site – nice and dry. Lovely views. Midges are quite thick but my repellant working well.

Today was hard at first but got easier/better. Managed to dump gash in a bin which lightened the lid of my pack (esp. of the heavy glass bottle from the Whisky – now decanted into small sigg). Again carefully staying away from pubs and tea rooms.

This bivi is beside a feeder stream into the Tees. Calming sound of water descending fast. Light is clear tonight. Makes me want to take photos. Have messaged home a lot since the first signal at Tan Hill. Now signal easy to get. Need to stop it. Feel much more relaxed about people in general up here. Fewer of them?

Monday 5th Sept. Tees Valley to Peeping Hill nr Dufton. 18m. 'Desperate Bivi'.

Monday am

Awake at 6.00. Awake on and off during night. Had hot drink and plenty of pemmican etc. but some hunger pangs in the night.

Many dreams during the night. One of trying to cross a river on what I thought was a bridge but it started to snap – made of elastic 'handrails' and a solid pole. Called to a man to help me (if he could) he said probably not. I asked him to try. He said a lot of idiots end up in the river downstream from doing this. I managed to get myself back and told him to F off. Another dream involved living in a house where the boiler was behind a wall and we thought it was exploding. Turned out to be a big cardboard arrow shooting through the wall with Egyptian symbolism on it and a hidden room behind. Too many cartoons as a child?

Woke to rain – still dark – and sensed/saw something. Didn't know whether hallucinating or whether something was moving slowly up the hill a metre or so away staring at me. Had impression of a red colour. Silent. Was momentarily bothered, searching the darkness, but soon settled down again. Comfortable night except for ankle soreness. Pressure sores on front of ankles that I don't seem to be able to relieve.

Washed my face and hands in stream in the morning and brushed my teeth. Felt good. Lots of sorrel and even some wild garlic still on the banks. Starting on to the North Pennines section today.

Monday pm

Stunning day. Threw everything at me. Beautiful, awesome waterfalls on Tees, Low Force and High Force, and slightly scary one at Cauldron Snout where the Tees kicks off as a substantial creature. Strange 'juniper garden' on hill overlooking High Force, on long walk along the river valley. Clamber over boulders round bend in river v. tiring on legs and slow, then wet scramble up hill alongside Cauldron Snout waterfall. V. Tenuous with pack on and tired legs. Two couples walking up PW as well. Kept criss-crossing. Noticed tracks on wet grass like tyre tracks and realised that I'd seen them everywhere, and that people walk in twos at such exact distance apart that looks like car track. When gets more arduous track becomes single again, then branches back into two. Had to stop self rushing to catch up all the time. It gets in my head badly. Remind myself all the time that I'm well equipped and will be fine if I'm careful and don't rush things.

Mist then rain, then very dense mist over Dufton Fell. Wrangle with myself over whether to push up on or find somewhere sheltered down in valley. Would mean staying there though. Long made-up (MOD) road into the fell (rubble). Surprised by size of Maize Beck on top of the Fell and glad of a bridge to get to north side. Unrelenting wind and clag as move over top along High Cup Nick. Very hard going with painful ankles. Sense of the drama but see virtually nothing. Should be able to see Lake District. Just ominous towers of rock and a drop-off in front of me. Got a bit concerned about making it off in daylight since the going so slow and laborious, but once on descent route it soon meets a made-up track into valley by Peeping Hill. Before that I went through lovely sheltered amphitheatre of good grass and rock walls. Thoughts to stop but lots of sheep. Have set up a 'desperate bivi' by an abandoned building. Very wet grass and sloping. BUT a good stream close by for refil.

Filter squeeze bottle sprang a leak and wet my trouser pocket, so wasn't pleasant. Have spare bottles. Setting up and fetching water I stumbled over two obstacles in exhaustion, so its fortunate that I have stopped for the night. Church bells in valley. Always enjoy that. Geese formation overhead. Talking to each other all the time. Love the sight and sound.

Wrecked and wretched though all the same.

Tuesday 6th Sept. Peeping Hill to Gregs Hut (Bothy) on Cross Fell. 10m.

Up at 6.30, left at 8.00. Couldn't get stove alight. V. Wet. Not feeling able to eat this morning or last night. Exertion? Makes me worry. Good spot though despite the slope. Need to take a lot of time to get properly repacked when in bivi.

Had a big day again in terms of conditions. Everything wet. Collected dead wood and thistle heads for the stove as I walked through very muddy, tree lined, path out of Dufton.

When reached side of Dufton Pike saw walkers ahead of me again and had to force myself to stay within myself, not rush to catch up. Realised that catching up a bad idea anyway coz then will either have to go faster or walk with/just behind them. Kept timing how far ahead they were. Made me think is the whole doing-it-alone thing my struggle with dependence over independence? V. Tough day. Started dry and relatively clear but low cloud over green fell and continuous clag over all the tops, despite high wind. From Knock Fell to Great Dunn Fell line of upright hollow poles/pipes. They sang in the wind like pan pipes – each different pitch. Atmospheric and ominous.

Extremely strong wind and v. Low visibility over Little Dunn Fell and Cross Fell. Had to pick my way v. carefully and take a compass bearing on cross Fell.

Path on Cross Fell travels over Boulder field so little to give a clue as to path when cloud down. Couldn't see cairns. Wind blowing pack over sideways. Felt lop-sided.

Met a few people coming and going from the Bothy, but saw nobody over cross fell. Ankles feeling the punishment now for a few days, esp on left foot. Raised lumps on fronts of ankles with bruising. Have been adjusting lacing, but don't want boots too loose and unstable. Feet are constantly immersed in water. Very boggy coming down cross fell.

Delighted when reached the path to the Bothy. Think I'd made up my mind on top of the fell to stay there, even though only early afternoon. Tried to dry things out outside Bothy in the wind but air too damp. Amazing variety of clouds and mists constantly whirling round the fell, but glimpses of a really sunny day in the valley.

A young athletic fella going super lightweight style from north to south direction stopped off in Bothy for a brew and, I think, the usual noodles type meal that people carry.

I started on my feet. Complete swab of Whisky – felt good. Then hypodermic lancing of all the huge bubbles of skin that had formed. Then clamped them down with micro pore to stop them filling up with liquid again. Usually works. Next took the knife to my boots and got rid of stiff patches on the tongues with the makers' emblem on them. Hoped this would fix my ankle issues.

Eventually got stove going. Had very strong coffee with whisky in it. Shock at first but then got into it! Very damp and dark in the hut but I've no complaints. Shelter is amazing when had none for days and days.

A couple arrived and told me they weren't going to impose and would be outside – I didn't mind them in the hut, but they didn't ask. They started putting up tent outside in the gale, but pole broken and after attempts to solve that they told me they were going to have to foist themselves on me in the hut after all. Going north to south like the last visitor, so had some useful info. on the route ahead of me. Their question to me though, whether the route south of here is very boggy, gave me a good clue that it was going to be hard going to the north. They, like me, prefer to sleep outdoors more than indoors. Carrying same weight as me but split between them. Shocked me when they started up a primus stove in the other room of the hut coz the noise was phenomenal. Bit worried about carbon monoxide but have decided it won't be on long enough to be a danger.

My things are all spread out on the sleeping platform – luxury to be able to sort through. Phone about half charged so tried to charge it but none left in powerpack. Bummer. 50% won't last so will have to try and charge in Alston. No adaptor plug with me though. Thinking round and round all the permutations.

Turned to planning rest of expedition. Very long days needed. A lot of pressure.

Damp sleeping bag but feels warm at the moment. Hoping for sun tomorrow. Been too long without sunlight. Can hear the wind howling around the Bothy. Like it.

Wednesday 7th Sept. Gregs Hut to Larchet Hill. 19m. 'Makey-Do' Bivi.

Up at 6am. Night was a bit frustrating coz v. Comfortable but one of our company snored. Wind outside was howling all night – learned from the couple (who learned it from the visitors book), that the fell has its own wind called the Helm Wind[22]. In the end tried to just enjoy being there and not bother about being awake. Could smell sauerkraut on sleeping bag and bivi bag and other bits. Realised had a spill, but checked it and lid still on. Build up of pressure had forced the gases and liquid out through the lid seal. Resolve to release sauerkraut pressure each day (burp it) and keep bottle upright. Have to get used to smelling a bit 'iff-ey'.

Poo – it is interesting that my poo now looks indistinguishable from the kind a wild animal would make. Dark, glossy, evenly shaped each time, inoffensive. Makes me think the rations might be quite near to what my body is designed to digest.

Got up as soon as enough light to pack. Others got up. Chat about pemmican. Also told me there was nothing in Byrness to stock up for Cheviots climb. Made me concerned. Not much pemmican left. Decided to get some salami and more dried fruit in Alston as a stop gap incase I needed emergency food on the mountain. Would hate to have to be rescued.[23] Filled out visitors book in bothy.

---

22 The Helm Wind occurs when a north-easterly blows across the south-west slope, creating a standing wave and a cloud cap (the Helm Bar). The same phenomenon occurs over some other UK mountains, but none of the others are named.

23 In the event this remained emergency food and unused, fortunately.

Walk down from hut long and easy. Feeling good. Convoy of 4x4 off up to the moor. Series of polite nods and good mornings was heart warming. Had a good sprightly pace. Visibility at last! Actually became quite hot quite quickly. Met an old chap in Garigill who gathered I had come from the hut. Helpfully pointed me to river ford for water.

Walk to Alston good in many places. Diversity of plants. Much good foraging. Still puzzled about lack of Apples and damson trees, and blackberries for that matter. But verges and meadows not all covered in nettles. Lots of elegant rowan trees.

Farmer mending dry stone wall in his underpants! Made me think how much time it takes and what it's like to allow yourself that – enough time to do a good job.

Collected dried spruce and cones for the stove – fingers crossed I can get them to burn.

Thought I must have overshot Alston coz waymarks dried up. Had been hearing traffic for ages. Felt I'd walked far enough. Pressed on after looking closely at footpath map.

Alston shops didn't look promising for buying a socket or getting phone charged somewhere. Bought salami and fruit from garage. Went to tourist info/library and librarian there lent me her iphone adaptor and let me charge phone in the lobby. Caught up with logbook. Took ages. Was hoping to charge the powerpack as well but left after an hour and ten minutes with 98% charge.

Feet have been playing up painfully. Pressure spots on heals and ankles. Feeling strong though. Love the accent here. Geordy is so melodic and interesting. See signs for Hexham and Durham. Come a long way! My walking has been a bit stop-start up to now. First this is wrong, then that needs attention, then pain in hip gets to me… but not so much today. Making myself attend to everything at one stop rather than lots of stops. On the hills, though, I do need to stop frequently to maintain myself. Would be very frustrating with a partner in a different rhythm. You'd never get anywhere. Maybe that's why people tend to drift apart and walk on their own (except the ones who make the parallel 'vehicle tracks').

Some nice interludes today. Looking at roman fort, whitley castle (from a distance) on stonking wooden bench designed for that purpose. Some horrid ones : getting stuck on old railway line, now cycle route, and having to double back.

Wednesday pm

Beginning to lose the point in it all. Can't get as far as I want. Having to bivi 5 miles short of planned distance. Really unsure what to expect in terms of availablity of places to stop. Makes it difficult to know when to stop. Took nearly 2 hours in Alston which is very annoying. Did enjoy the Tyne river today very much, but got really tired with silly routes through little fields plowed into sludge by cattle – very hard on my white and mushy feet and infection worry with open sores. Want to keep my feet on the flat all the time but impossible. Just when I needed to get going and make mileage a really stupid bit after Slaggyford, taking detours round fields and eventually (when I doubled back time and again to find the route) it took me over a wall into somones back yard right by their conservatory window. Couldnt see my way out, which turned out to be using a stone jutting out in middle of the wall. Felt like a puzzle or game getting through there. Few indications of others going through that way, so I wonder!

Feeling down. Maybe just fagged out. Was looking forward to walking along the roman road after burnstones, but turns out there isn't one. That phrase (site of) should warn me. Set up bivi on moorland (Larchet hill) quite close to a farm and within sound of road. Just using bivi bag, no tarp. 'Makey-do bivi'.

Thursday 8th Sept. Larchet Hill to Peel. 17m. Mindful Bivi

Thursday am

Awake at 6am looking at a red sky. Okay so more rain then. Thought it was going to rain last night when settled and that I would lie here in my self pity getting soaked, but it was just the dew falling. Skies cleared and I could see the stars for the first time this leg. Slept well but had periods of wakefulness. Full of concern over whether I can finish and struggle with myself over how hard I can push. Pain in my left arm (and so it has come!) I am thinking about whether this might be incipient heart attack, especially given pain in the jaw too. But then my jaw hurts because I grind my teeth at night, and pain in my arm is to be expectd carrying such weight and using a pole in left hand for the first time.

This Morning I feel more philosophical and relaxed about the final few days that I have before stopping. I wont kill myself but I WILL try hard. I am feeling very grotty which I dont think is helping, so in spite of guilt over time wasting Im going to wash my underwear in the stream as soon as I reach it. Couldnt face food last night except a bit of dried fruit but this morning will have some pemmican.

The huge spider in the grass – looming above me last night – has gone now and seems to have taken its web with it. The slug who was making for my food has also gone. The grouse have been in great numbers and up close all evening and since dawn this morning. Very noisy. Lovely. The stile over my wall is one of those wooden ladders either side that cross over into handrails at the top. Most are like that now. They look like birds perched on the top of the walls.

Thursday pm

Walked to the end of the Hadrians wall section of the route. Stopped 7pm. Went all day no breaks. Heaving rain coming over the moors up to and beyond A69 crossing. BUT was enjoying it and relaxed on the moors. The expanses seem to soothe my mind. Anyhow you have to forget worries when in water up to your shins! Sun came out just before A69 crossing and I took shelter in an old house/cattle shed to swap clothes. As soon as I got going again so did rain.

Waymarkers haven't been good today. Feet very blistered – having to check them out every day and treat. Walking in bogs helps coz you get to not feel them, but dangerous. Have been too hot at night so far, but have a feeling that tonight not so. Was very exposed on the escarpment and I was being blown over. Was looking forward to coffee and Whisky tonight but don't really feel like it now. Perhaps will make it anyhow.

Have a LOT of miles to cover tommorow if want to give myself a chance of getting to Kirk Yetholm. Need suitable weather. Sun setting now. Looks promising colour. Red sky this morning was entirely accurate. Let's hope tonight's sky is so. Happy with myself for not quitting at YHA in Twice Brewed. Instead went to other side of the escarpment and found trees for shelter.

Friday 9th Sept. Peel to Highstead Hill nr Bellingham. 17m. Tepee Bivi.

Friday 5.50am

Was so tired last night that gave up lighting fire in semi-darkeness. Wind picked up dramatically over night and buffeted my tarp even under cover of trees and a wall. Could hear it rumbling along/over the crags. Had a couple of spells of rain and got out to adjust basha/tarp.

Early evening the crows started roosting in trees above me and brought that unique atmosphere that crows do. They settled to quietness. Had lots of dreams to do I think with not respecting people's property. A doctor lent me some state-of-the-art glasses that picked up radio/ music, and I used the case to collect water.

More disturbingly I helped a girl to bury a dead relative because she said it had all been taken out of her hands. Woke up and it was completely still – no wind. Looking up at the trees I started to think about the dreams and try to explain them to myself and found myself in tears. Made me wonder, after I'd stopped crying, whether the other person I'm always talking to (talking to myself) sort of explaining myself to, whether its a similar feeling that people have getting comfort from God. An experience of omnipresence.

Always knew to do a walk like this has to be a form of therapy, but now not sure how much of it is beyond what I'm aware of. Also thought for first time that maybe mountains arent the be-all for me and that forests are more so. Looking straight up at tall trees is profound. Also thought about why I ended up working in psychology. I suppose I muse a lot about meaning, but so do writers and poets and thats my realm really – the particular not the general. Also doing this has something to do with getting older and feeling the urgency of seeing things through.

Friday pm

Been mentally challenging day for me today, even though physically I'm quite strong. I don't seem to notice my mangled feet too badly. Was up at 6,00, left at 7.00 and walked pretty much non stop to Bellingham where I stopped under a river bridge for food/water and a think. Want so badly to succeed, but really not poss to get to kirk yetholm. Even thought of walking through the night at one point. Tonight thinking maybe I could get up to the first refuge on Lamb's Hill tomorrow from here and down to Kirk Yetholm on Sunday. Will have to see how I go with the bogs tomorrow. Looks as though the walk through the Keilder forest is on forest roads.

The walk through Wark Forest Today was difficult – unexpectedly. The path cut across the forest roads, and the terrain in between was muddy and swampy. There are continous swerving paths of rushes flattened down, like waves, where walkers have used it to try and avoid sinking in the mush. walked through a section of moorland enclosed on three sides by the forset. Wonderful rainbow behind me and I could see the cloud advancing. Was on me quickly. Stopped at a ruin to get poncho wrapped aound pack and put on waterproofs. Took ages. When I turned around lots of fluffy faces watching me intently. Calves. Very cute but potentially my nemesis. I couldn't see their mothers through the group but very quietly moved in a big circle away from them. Have had to make a lot of exaggerated route adaptations for calves, cows and bulls. There really are a lot of all three. Not so many sheep at all.

Been a superb foraging day – finally! Blackberries, bilberries, but still no apples. But what there is tons of up here is sorrel – not the little leaves but huge generous ones. Had to stop myself just eating and eating, involving stopping and stopping. Collected some up though to snack on. Like having sweets – takes away dryness in mouth.

Was so tempted today by all the treats on the way. Like pot of tea on the go at a farm (so said a sign), and notice at bottom of ravine that refreshments available at top. Campsite signs everywhere. Need to stick to my guns.

Really enjoyed being on the high tops but rain threatening all the time so have made a habit now of strapping poncho over pack with paracord and wearing my goretex (when I can bear the heat), or having it over my shoulder for easy access. Have made quite a few adaptations to poncho and pack, removing things here and adding them there.

As I write (in my bivi) I swear I can hear music in a car thumping but cut off here and no buildings for miles. Only a bridleway. Thats why I chose it. Bogs are everywhere here: on the tops, in the dips and on the slopes – no getting away from them. Used to pick my way around them but takes too long. Now just march headlong through mostly.

POLES – used to the necessity of poles in the Alps for testing snow and crevasses, but on this stretch at least necessary for testing bogs.

Bellingham seems a very nice place but had a bit of stand-offishness. Realising I look more like a hobo now than whatever it was I thought I looked like. Keep thinking "yes I know, but I'm doing the Pennine Way y'know". My three pronged pole probably has a bit of an impact. Just a useful thing but looks totemic so makes people nervous. Who/what do I think I am?

I'm on a high knoll just beyond Bellingham with wind gusting strongly. Scots pine in a walled area and a sycamore. Constructed a tepee type arrangement from the poncho. Three pronged pole essential!

No phone signal. Bugger. Need to start arranging my lift out with sister.

Saturday 10th Sept. Bellingham to border fence on Cheviots. 19m. Border Bivi.

Saturday am

Its 5.30. Very wet and windy night. Slept okay. Was thinking about the couple in Gregs Hut carrying about the same weight as me but sharing. That's how people do it when they camp on the move. But seems to me danger of staying within relationship bubble. Can't help it. Don't then have the vulnerability that I want – the thing that makes it really hard and keeps me trying.

Have decided this morning that everything points me to finishing in Byrness. Pemmican running out, weather awful, blisters and sores, too little time – meaning I'd finish so late my sister and mum would have to drive through the night to get everyone home for work Monday. I might get into needless difficulty which is not the purpose. What it does mean is that for the next leg to Knoydart

I'll need to start with the Cheviots, so Ill have wet feet and gear from day one.

It's really astonished me that despite spells of sun and plenty of wind I've been completely unable to dry my socks. Maybe marsh water lingers the longest. Waiting now for enough daylight to operate in. The wind and rain has stopped – the lull before the dawn – but often starts up again once its paused for sunrise

Saturday pm

Was up at 6am. Left 7ish. Been quite hard going around Keilder Forest today. Before that, slipped over for the first time in the muddy slopes on Deer Play hill. Didn't mind the hills despite the slipperiness. Sandstone showing through. Steep, muddy slope up to the forest then a hateful yomp through even worse swamps than yet. And proper bog – flat surface of peat/soil that I stepped on and leg sank right in. Couldn't get it out. Boot stayed on but didn't think it would. Feeling iff'y about forests now. Sitting here after just getting to the forest road met a guy doing the whole thing from Edale to Kirk Yetholm in 10 days – for charity. Camping on the way. Looked in good spirits and pretty strong. Started to feel my effort measly.

Saturday pm later

Foraging continued today. Feel as though it's been a double day because of last minute change of plan. Had resigned myself to finishing in Byrness, but weather good, feeling strong, continued onto Cheviots. Went to the border fence. Delights me. This is success – now made it to Scotland. The weather was so stable I thought a night on the hills wouldn't be too bad. Bivi is set now and quite cold up here but cosy in my sleeping bag. Very little wind. At

Keilder forest I was excited to get to the forest road but turned out not to be a happy relationship. For miles and miles it's slopes are covered in fir trees that have thick foliage to the ground. All very uniform. Dense planting. Feels dead. More barren than the moors. The dead quality of the forest had another bad effect. Man who was behind me for quite a way suddenly picked up speed and overtook me then kept looking back at me. He was only dressed in day gear so not doing Pennine Way even though on the route. Made me quite nervous. Then when got down to the river realised there were lots of folk around – it's a park with a visitor centre and all that. Not sure about that man but the atmosphere of this forest borders on sinister. Notices telling you you are being watched, cctv notices, notices warning vandals to refrain from wrecking bothies, measures to block vehicle access.

When walking beside the river I felt more relaxed. A couple walking their dog hailed me to comment on me having a hazel pole. The gent also carried hazel. He had same thoughts as me about its qualities and also indispensibility around the bogs. His was posh with a buffalo finial, but it didnt seem to matter. Cheered me up a lot.

Jaunty now. Headed straight up onto the Cheviots (mud slope then rocky scramble). More MOD land to watch out about. Bullets draped over a fence. Notices to keep the right side of the military ranges. Notices not to touch any ordnance. Strange feeling.

GLORIOUS weather. Just a few hours on from the valley and I'm on on the border. Made it to Scotland!

No water tonight but have my sauerkraut which is actually more refreshing. Thought I might make gypsy well, but no need[24]

---

24 A Gypsy Well is a method for getting clean water from wet ground by digging a hole and using tightly packed bundles of grass in the hole to filter the water that seeps back into it. After the water has been emptied out a few times it becomes clean enough to use – either as it is or boiled, depending on the water source.

Sunday 11th Sept. Cheviots to Byrness. 5m

Sunday am

Very comfortable night due to thick grasses and mosses under me. Found myself a cluster of three small fir trees to nest inside. Could hear wind whipping up all night. Sounded high above and below in valley at the same time but didnt impact on where I was sleeping. Maybe was being whipped up the valley and over my head?. Perfect spot then – but not due to cleverness. Had rain intermittantly. Initially extremely cold. Ended up using cacoon sleeping bag liner – so not carried in vain. Warmed up enough to stop having the shakes. Sky was clear in between showers and could see milky way and shooting stars. Stars very bright but was having difficulty picking out constellations – in the end wondered why I was trying to. Mosquito just landed on my hand but didnt bite. I've rubbed my spruce resin balm on my hands and neck and seems as though it's worked as a repellant[25]. I love the smell – vast improvememt on smell of socks.

Pack has developed a whole range of conversation now beyond the monosyllabic squeaks. Most of the time yesterday though it was telling me to dig deep. Feel a great affection for all my gear. It seems natural to think more superstitiously on my walks – thoughts or responses come to me and I accept them with a sideways glance, knowing they aren't exactly rational. They are my interaction with the world. I don't think any less of them for that. Rationality doesn't get you very far in extremis. There's something in your body that you talk to and feel with.

This morning a red sky that has now been quickly covered in clouds. So be it, I suppose. Hope the wind gets up and blows them away.

Going to take Border County Ride trail back down through

---

25 I made the balm from resin that I collected from the trunks of spruce and pine trees (they produce more than they need to heal rents to the bark). I melted the resin and filtered it, then combined it with beeswax and oil.

the forest to Byrness. Have no water now but looks like we cross streams on this route.

Sunday 10.00 am

Last log. Walked down the Heads Toe track instead of Border County Ride, coming out on Jedburgh road. Glad, because avoids scramble down wet crags and all the mud of the ascent route. Stopped at Byrness church. Weather turned to rain on the tops before I struck camp so moved out quickly without bothering about pack organisation. Letting go of discipline now its ending. Felt quite emotional and tearful on descent. Helped by sighting group of deer who kept reappearing ahead of me. Water difficult to get coz river very cut-in and also gullies dredged deeply. Found a nice rivulet coming down from forest running into sand/clay channel. Completely clear. Took some.

Just waiting at the church in the sunshine. Nip of Whisky for me and one for the nineteenth century curate whose gravestone I'm sitting on.

Things I won't take next time

There are a few things I won't take next time that add up to a kilo at most. I overdid the clothes, having two short sleeves and two long sleeves, so I'll leave one of each. Two jackets is also probably overdoing it, and so I'll either take the primaloft or the fleece. My gaiters weren't much use so depending on the season will probably leave them. Other than that I overdid only the medications, with plasters and far too many diorylite sachets. If you injure yourself either you need a proper dressing or none at all, not a plaster at any rate, and if I need that much diorylite then I probably need to come home! Some weight was down to bad planning, finding myself with only a heavy pair of scissors for example. My striker (ferro rod) is very large and heavy so I'll take a much smaller one. I also have a few needlessly heavy clips and attachments I can jettison and use cord instead. Seriously thinking of a lighter weight pack that will dry out quickly, and a lightweight cover. Wary of getting too 'technical' though and changing the nature of my expedition.

Postscript

Was at work Monday, but with bad oedema in the lower legs/feet. Strapped them up and raised them overnight which helped a bit. My poor feet took a lot of injuries. Need to look into boots for bogs and for people with bunions, ready for Part Four.

5

Expedition Part Four: 'Crazy Leg', May 2017

This stage has been coined my 'crazy leg', not for the ambitions of it so much as the mental states it induced. The worry that I was faced with on the journey back to Byrness, and when I had to finally step from the car and walk away, had been avoided up until then in the planning and preparing.

The bad weather leg caused me to think carefully about the perils of setting out for 320 miles through Scotland with the same kit. I didn't want to try and spend my way out of hardship, because there's no end to that kind of solution, but I knew that my feet needed more care, and that for a heavier load I would have to use a more suitable pack. I wasn't going to be able to make boots nor a rucksack, but these were very generously bought and gifted to me by family. On the other hand, I *could* have a go at making a new bivi bag and basha, couldn't I? I enjoyed that, as an idea and a process, but it has to be said that at least one member of the WI (Women's Institute) has since laughed at the stitching and puzzled over how my bivi bag managed to keep me dry.

Blog entry 22nd Feb 17

Just seven weeks to go before I leave. I feel more excited than worried this time, which is disconcerting – and starting to worry me! The distance I need to cover is much further than either of the legs already completed, and my rations will be even more pared-down. April in Scotland is a bit of a gamble, since snow and cold could knock me back. Till now, though, spring has been my favoured season so I hope for the same again.

Blog entry 1st March 17. Material Changes: Getting into Fabrics

A few things I have treated myself to are: (1) a new pair of mountain boots that are designed for feet with bunions (if my feet get damaged as much as last time I won't make the distance, so they are make-or-break), (2) the other new thing is a pack that doesn't absorb water and fits my back better (female design). It is 65 litres capacity rather than 70 so that is a concern with having to carry so much more pemmican and sauerkraut. The foraging won't be very good so early in the year so I need to be careful that I carry enough. The other thing about spring is a lack of good leaf cover of course, but so far on the expedition that's not been too difficult to get around – though there are stretches along the South of Scotland that will be quite urban.

My bivi bag and poncho/tarp/basha have seen better days and the bag is quite leaky, so I'm making new ones. Great fun! I might have been a bit too generous with the size of the bag for my legs, but I would rather that than suffer the pain of an immobile hip. Looking forward to trying it out in a week or so when it's finished. The basha is finished now, in a neat 7-sided design that seems to work really well.[26]

---

26   It took me a while to decide on the fabrics to use for each. For the basha I went for

Blog Entry 3rd March 2017: Busy Busy

Writing is the last thing I want to do at the moment. I'm busy: testing kit, making kit, prepping food, finding stuff that I used last time that I now regret putting away, and planning my route. When I'm busy I don't want to stop: not even to write. But I need to have a record of what I'm up to so I can recall it when I need it again.

There are some new things this time that I'm trying. I've mentioned that I'm making my tarp and bivy bag – going well so far – and I'm probably going to use off-cuts from the tarp to make some new gaiters.

Sauerkraut, Pemmican and Tallow: Further Developments

Making my own expedition food (sauerkraut and pemmican) is second-nature now. To test myself further with self-reliance this time, though, I'm making a starter culture for my sauerkraut from raw (unpasteurised) milk. It's the whey that I need (as in curds and whey).

Being fortunate enough to be able to get some raw milk, we've been having a lot of fun at home. You can do things with raw

---

very lightweight ripstop nylon with silicone coating. It's really slippery, especially against itself, so you have to avoid treading on it, but water almost jumps off it. The design was hard-won, since I wanted it wider than the size available so had to decide where to put the seam so as not to compromise the waterproofing too much. The seven sides make for a more suitable shape than a rectangle for adapting to different locations and for stringing it between walking poles.

For the bivi bag I wanted a breathable waterproof fabric that wasn't too heavy. I chose coated microfibre, which has a soft outer and shiny inner side, and cobbled a design that would open at the top rather than from a side seam, and would have an adjustable hood. I had to figure out the best way to keep it reasonably waterproof without sealing the seams, since taping is fiddly and in my experience doesn't work too well on a DIY basis. The most important factor for the design was to have it wide enough for me to move my legs around so that I could potentially get relief from the pain in my hip.

milk that you can't do with pasteurised milk, because the helpful microbes aren't dead. All you have to do is leave it to separate and sour, which produces cream, yoghurt, butter, cheese and whey. We made some butter in less than 20 minutes this morning from the soured cream. What came as a revelation to me is that the acids produced when you let the milk sour actually extend the 'shelf-life' of the raw milk products. When milk is pasteurised, though, it just goes toxic when it sours.

It's the whey that I want for my sauerkraut, to start the fermentation process. You *can* make sauerkraut without it, as I did before – the microbes on the cabbage and in the air will do it – but more slowly and with a more mild result. It'd be really tragic to get a contaminated batch, as I did last time, so I plan to be really careful with cleaning the pot and keeping the water seal on the pot full. Mould grew because the water-seal dried up. It probably wouldn't have been harmful but the sauerkraut tasted off, so I didn't use it.

I used to use beef kidney fat for my pemmican but last time I preferred using scraps of fat taken from ordinary cuts of beef for the taste and texture. So I have some tallow left over from the first expedition that I might use to make some soap to take with me. That would be really satisfying. In the processing time I have left I might only be able to make soft soap, but that will do. All you need is lye (leached from hard wood ashes) and fat (my tallow), and heat. The acid (fatty acids) react with the alkali (lye) to make a salt (soap) and glycerol. You just need time to let it set and to make sure all the lye has reacted with the fat, otherwise it could be caustic.

On the more prosaic side of things my physical state is a worry. The hip is quite limiting at the moment (painful to walk on), and the knee is acting up again because of it. I have another injection into the hip booked in two weeks' time, which I am relying on to see me right for the expedition, otherwise it doesn't look promising. As before, though, I just have to get on with preparing and trust to things turning out well. I've set a date and place (Sat 6th May at

Inverie or Mallaig) to be met by my sister for a lift out, so reality now bites!

Blog entry, 15th March 2017

This is my medical week: tomorrow the check-up at the spinal hospital, and Sunday my hip injection. All attention on the body! I know the break site in my back is deteriorating, from the X-ray they did last time, but I don't envisage anything that will stop my expedition. The hip damage is a known quantity too. It's been playing up – painful – making me nervous. I *have* managed to walk through bad attacks before, so even if the injection doesn't work I still have a chance. Grit is the key, but how much do I have? It's a question that never goes away.

I have two distinct hopes about my expedition: that it's really hard and that it's not hard at all. Gleefully rejecting comforts as I pack my rucksack I then fret over what I *could* have packed that might help me succeed. Travelling light is a good policy from most points of view, so at least I have that as a rationale for walking a thin line.

I'm not a survivalist trying to prepare for the end of civilisation – that's not why I keep paring back the layers of comfort and convenience with each stage. But there *is* something anti-social in me, and I sometimes feel futility in the ease of the day-to-day. That's what makes me, in my middle class, middle aged environs, feel helpless. I think for a woman it's rare – historically and as a rule – to be able to make the main decisions: the ones of consequence. But it's vital. The thing about the expeditionary life is that every action *does* have consequences that you care about. Life becomes much simpler travelling alone, and it stamps out the nonsense of fearing phantoms, bugs and beasts. The only thing you have to fear is your own bad choices. That is especially true of choices related to other people.

The things you have to gain are far more important than what you have to lose. You *are* in a meaningful environment, because it rains on you, shines on you, includes you in the turning of the planet through daylight to night and out the other side. You might suffer, but you'll probably survive and be better off. If you don't survive you will have existed.

This is the opposite to Wells' apocalyptic story, 'War of the Worlds', where the threats are unequivocal, entirely external and beyond any human influence. Though I have to note that in the end the planet saved itself and belonged to itself again.

So it comes to this then: I have to conclude that I have something to prove to myself, and I become most happy when I test myself against it: my existence.

Blog entry 28th March 2017

Only two weeks to go. I feel shocking though. There's some kind of cold bubbling along in my body that's sapping my energy and giving me night sweats. The inflammation makes everything sore and is bothering my hip too, so whilst I've had my steroid injection I'm not feeling the benefit. It's discouraging. It makes me worry about deterioration in my fitness, since I don't feel exercise is the right thing with the current symptoms. The mantra that 'I've felt worse before and it worked out' is all I have to go on.

My check up at the hospital has put me in line for another MRI because of some loss of sensation and cramps in my foot. I'll be having that when I get back from my expedition.

Pemmican and Sauerkraut Inspiration

On a more inspiring note, the food prep is going nicely. Our butcher, Kevin, put aside a couple of kilos of fat and beef for my pemmican, so that's underway. I've made jerky with the beef (just sliced it thinly and left it in the oven on a very low heat for 24 hours). Now I need to render the fat.

The sauerkraut was burping gas nicely, so hadn't died off, and I decided to have a taste. It is absolutely wonderful. When I took the lid off the smell was fresh and the liquid over the weight blocks was clear, apart from a very small milky film over the blocks, which is a harmless and normal growth. What was a complete surprise is how minty the flavour is. The caraway seeds, which were a bit of a gamble, seem to have produced this great taste. I've bottled it and put it in the fridge so as to slow down the fermentation.

Andy has started a new batch off with juniper berries, which has now produced some bubbles. If the house is warm enough it should be ready by the time I leave, supplementing my supply.[27]

My plan is to carry the sauerkraut in water bladders, put into tough plastic bags as secondary waterproofing. I've bought two 1.5 ltr bladders that have open tops with waterproof closures. The idea is that they'll be tough enough to carry liquid, easy enough to open up, and easy to release the fermentation gasses from through the valve. I've cut the hoses right down so they don't get in the way.

The next job is to repair the seams and pocket of my goretex jacket and make some clothing selections based on the long range weather forecasts.

Blog Entry 4th April 2017

There's now one week remaining. This settled weather is just what I would like for my expedition, but it has come too early for me. The May downturn looks like coming sooner this year, so I'm most likely going to be starting out over the Cheviots in the wet, or even the

---

27   Unfortunately this went horribly bad and was left in the croc pot until July since nobody wanted the job of disposal. After several washes the croc still smells strange.

snow. That'll be hard, especially if things don't pick up. Spending too long soaking wet is dismal.

Today I went to the gym for the first time in a month. It is the only time I can recall going easy on a session. I'm really trying to look on the positive side of things but my health is still a worry. At night I've had sweats and vomiting and difficulty breathing, with no appetite in the day and a feeling of dehydration. When I eat a meal it makes me feel ill. Added to that I have some bites on my legs and torso, as well as a rash on my arm that itches and isn't going away. I don't think the two are connected, but the combined effect makes my skin crawl. After fumigating the bedroom for fleas and bedbugs, incase it was one or other, the bites have lessened but the patch of dermatitis/eczema/whatever won't shift.

That alone spurs me on to get outside so I don't have to live with the microorganisms that share the house – that share my bed! It has to be healthier to live as a nomad rather than in situ with a burgeoning population of cosseted parasites. Given that over-cleaning is as unhealthy as over-crowding, the answer to unsanitary living conditions should be to spread out more and move about, not just perform ever more industrial cleansing.

So, coming back to the main theme here, whilst I should be keeping up my fitness I've shied away from exercise, thinking that I might do myself more harm than good. Thankfully the hip pain has reduced, which adds to my feeling of wanting to rest so as not to set it off.

Will I be embarking on this expedition completely unfit, and possibly diseased?

Logbook: Written in the Raw

Thursday 13th April 2017. Border Fence to Chew Green Bivi.

Travelled up with Andy from home to Byrness, Northumberland, where the Expedition stopped last September. Was up at 6am and out the door by 6.30. We slept in the cabin in the garden so as not to wake everyone (mainly so as not to wake animals). Faffy dog ended up with us in the cabin last night. Was nice and warm in there and useful for getting used to bedding down on hard surface.

Took until 1.30pm to drive up to the starting point. Good journey with alternating feelings of relaxation, enjoying the view and feeling nostalgic about the territory I'd already walked through, and silent anxiety about what I was headed for.

When we reached Byrness had difficulty recognising the route I'd taken to get off the Cheviots. Finally decided on a forestry path and said goodbye to Andy. Felt very novice stood there having picture taken.

The route up onto the tops didn't look at all how I'd remembered it when I was coming down – lots of sawn tree trunks – quite desolate looking. But when I turned around and looked back down I recognised the view. Before it had seemed quite verdant and I was enjoying the sight of deer ahead of me, but I suppose winter had intervened, and that was at the end of an arduous few weeks not the beginning of something even longer. Was reassured that on the right path by seeing the Bothy/cabin perched on the opposite hillside that made such an impression on me before.

The pack felt heavy and my hip hurt. The hip strap of my new pack seems to slip loose all the time. Feel quite fumbly. Once back at my high point of last year, I decided to take the slightly longer route onwards – a dogleg out to Chew Green Roman Camp (extensive raised earth mounds) – and have set up bivi here. Not very happy with my tarp arrangement – too few pegs to make it work by stretching it between my walking poles so I've used my trowel as one peg and letting one of the loops flap free in the wind. Have SOME shelter from the side of an earth mound but not much. Luckily no wind.

Hip hurt when walking quite a bit but just trusting it'll settle down. Have no idea how my bivi bag will perform. Think I might not get in it tonight unless it gets very cold – which it very well might! If I don't use it at least that will prevent condensation wetting sleeping bag. Have brought my cacoon sleeping bag liner which I might use.

Wish I didn't feel so inept.

Looking down to the Coquet stream and Dere Street (old Roman road) on opposite hillside. Many warning signs and military shooting/ shelter constructions. It's 8 miles from here to Windy Gyle (ominous name!) – a mile from there to Border Gate where many doing the route choose to wild camp because it's half way across the Cheviot route. I've only come 4.5m today. Seen a couple heading onwards and notice on my map that the first mountain refuge at Lamb Hill is only 3.5 miles away, but I don't want to cop out of my first night outside and take shelter – nor share my first night if the couple are headed there.

The sun just came out (5.20pm) but there are also a few rain clouds about. Maybe I'll get inside bivi bag tonight just in case?

Haven't been feeling hungry at all, so not sure whether I'll have anything tonight. Had a pie and cake at lunch at Tebay services so probably don't need anything anyhow.

Have been feeling VERY unsure about this. Felt much harder to leave the car (and Andy) than to take a train and start walking as I did at Hawes in September.

Have a sore spot on my middle toe, left foot, which is one reason why I think a very short day is in order to begin with. Don't want to do myself in so early on.

Good Friday, 14th April 2017

Chew Green to side of Black Hag. 'Good Friday Bivi'.

Bivi last night at Chew Green. Messed about for ages getting camp set so was glad to have stopped walking so early. Decided to use the bivi bag and found it really comfy and a reassuring thickness. Was VERY good to have a hood on it so I could look out while still wrapped up warm. Became VERY windy so eventually the noise of the tarp flapping got so annoying that I got out and released the guy attaching the foot end of the tarp to my other walking pole and just pegged it out at ground level.

It clouded over for quite a few hours and rained lightly on and off. Used walking boots to lift my head off the ground and put pack at my feet because started slipping downwards. Worked well. Long night – slept on and off. Clouds cleared and stars came out. VERY cold on my face but body stayed quite warm. Could feel my toe hurting – VERY BAD so early on!

Currently at mountain refuge hut on Lamb Hill having left camp at 7.00 and arrived here at 9.00. Can hear red grouse – lovely. Dawn chorus this morning very interesting. A sound like a deep vibration that moved eerily around the hillside making ooooooohhh noise (ghostly). Heard lapwings, grouse and many songbirds. Enjoyed listening.

Didn't want to get up but glad when had. Ate a bit a sauerkraut, and a few hazelnuts and prunes.

Quite a lot of water on tarp but could just shake it off. Magic!

The walk to the hut was hard. Left shoulder sore. But felt like a very familiar feeling. GOOD. LOVE THE EMPTY HILLS. Got a good view of the Eildon Hills I'm headed for on the Saint Cuthbert's Way, once I've reached Kirk Yetholm.

Hip not too bad now it is warmed up but twinges every so often. The sticks are essential.

It's 3.00ish and I'm now at Auchope Mountain Hut and considering my options. Too early to consider stopping here, but the weather has got up a bit. Saw a couple outside hut from a distance but they left prior to me getting here. Good. Hut is the same as Lamb Hill – basic but nicely kept. Benches around the walls. Not damp (like Cross Fell Bothy in the Autumn). But much smaller and just benches.

Today the morning miles seemed to go on forever, but pm has been good. Long/sharp pull over the Cheviot massif – v.v. slowly done. Heard several red grouse and more songbirds as well. The ground is nowhere near as bad as last September – much drier, so I haven't sunk too deep in anything. I suppose the weather has been quite dry, and with it being early in the season, and not too badly trodden, the ground hasn't been turned too mushy.

VERY WINDY this afternoon coming down to Auchope at Hen Hole. Nearly lost buff off my head and pack rain cover – added to which the wind kept slapping bits of my jacket into my face. Reminds me of how I used to feel in the Cairngorms in Winter.

When/if the weather abates going to head towards Kirk Yetholm and try and find available trees to settle under. Might make phone contact so I won't need to tonight. Feel I should at least let Andy know that walk is underway now. I'm looking at a notice on the wall giving Mounthooly WiFi password (joke?).

Incidentally the new, untried selfie stick broke this am. Well, I never really held with that idea anyway.

RAIN now outside. Will stay put for a while.

It's now 7.30pm. I've yomped down off my route to a forest for the night. Many fallen trees. High wind. Creaking everywhere. Complicated getting into forest over fences. Very dense right to the ground. Found suitable opportunity. Set up bivi at 6pm, just in time before the rain.

Have taken the chance to strip off, clean and change – feel better for that. Put dry sleeping clothes on for tonight. Will have a sip of whisky, a bite of pemmican, then off to sleep when it gets dark. VERY COLD. Wearing duvet jacket and down booties.

Saturday 15th April

Good Friday Bivi to Wether Hill, nr Morebattle. 'Fat Burning Bivi'

The night was very cold and extremely windy. Ended up putting duvet jacket and duvet boots back on inside my sleeping bag. The sound in the forest was deafening at times (wind on the forest sounds like a waterfall), and the trees creaked and groaned. Got quite worried about a collapse. Decided to turn on phone so that if anything happened to me I could be found.

Fitful bursts of sleep in between loud gusty spells. Comfortable, but I had difficulty getting that way (i.e comfortable).

Woke at 5.30am and started getting fixed to go, but wasn't out till 7.30 because of trying not to get too cold. Was joined by a Robbin (fat) who followed me about as I packed. Gave him a ball of pemmy fat. I'm finding my pemmican too fatty so will have to take time picking the meat out of it.

Had the hard climb out over barbed wire and back up through the heather to the prow of the hill to regain the Pennine way. Glad to take the lowland route then to Kirk Yetholm (basically just descending). Did my first foraging – gorse buds very sweet at the moment (early in season). Plenty of sorrel once I'd got down to the tracks.

In Kirk Yetholm now. 11.15am. Done about 5m. Church bell peels. Good feeling. Spurs me on. Kirk Yetholm bigger than I imagined. Came as a shock to hear all Scottish accents now. Still very cold/windy. Dumped selfie stick and gash in bin (kept Bluetooth controller from selfie stick). Seen a board with both the Pennine way and St. Cuthbert's Way, former advises compass, map reading ability, mountain equipment etc. whereas latter talks of lovely views, churches and tea shops. Will now be taking St. Cuthbert's Way to Melrose. No teashops for me though!

It was good to leave the Cheviots, though I enjoyed them I think, but St Cuthbert's Way has soon led me to some quite strenuous hill climbing over Crookedshaws and Wideopen Hill- every bit as hard as some of the Cheviot sections but dry underfoot thankfully. Saw more people on this trail. Was VERY windy again, interspersed with showers and very intense sun, so a bit annoying having to stop all the time to adjust clothing. Getting cold a bad idea, getting wet equally awful, so I don't like to risk sweating when it's warm or I'm working hard incase I'll be left in wet clothes.

Doing it this way (sleeping out) takes a long time because you have to look after every little bit of it and not say "that'll do" or "I'll just get wet then". Likewise I'm having to stop early in the day to have enough daylight with warmth in it to make an adequate bivi. I'm so aware of how far I have to go, can't let things slip.

For lunch I had to MAKE myself eat the pemmy. By picking the meat out of the huge volume of fat I can at least eat it.

Lots of calves and cows in the fields today. Had a few 'almost' encounters. I think the really big pack and sticks make me look strange/threatening. One particular cow was completely fixated on me to the point that I didn't want to get into the field. After I'd sat for a while I spotted her small calf asleep near the stile. Whatever she did it didn't move, so at last I had to get in with them and try to walk wide of the path. Farm had set up birthing pens in the quarry, which I walked around from above – secure walls of rock all round, and pens made of bales of straw. Cows looked very snug.

Stopped earlier than intended because riverside beautiful and lots of wild garlic beside scurrying stream. The rocks in the stream are all white, just like the walls, but seems to be white lichen covering everything rather than white geology. Crags look like the Roaches – gritstone.

Decided to have a hot drink and found the left-over paper from around the pemmican burns really hot (why not – like tallow candles). Foraging today: common sorrel, sheep sorrel, ransom (wild garlic), wood sorrel, gorse flowers/buds.

Tractors on slopes above bivi and cars and tractors on fields and roads beside me. Nice site though, below Wether Hill. Old fire pit here. Glad to have stopped early – 4pm – since it's given me time to set up well and DON'T WANT TO GO TOO HARD TOO SOON. Must keep eating but difficult. Will try to collect more leaves to supplement supplies and pep them up a bit more. ISSUES ARE JUST LIKE BEING AT ALTITUDE AGAIN.

MILEAGE:
CHEVIOTS APPROX 25M
5.5 M TO BIVI
= 30.5M IN 2 DAYS
FRIDAY 14TH – FRIDAY 6TH MAY = 21 DAYS
320M TO GO = 16M/DAY ESSENTIAL

Easter Sunday 16th April. Morebattle to Dere Street: 'Easter Sunday'
Bivi

Absolutely pooped today. Left Bivi 3 at 7.30am after getting up at
6.00. Night was blissful – long sleep. Very cosy now I've decided
to use sleeping bag liner (cacoon). Walking today painful to begin
with, which eased in spite of strenuous effort to carry. Was a relief to
be on easy ground and the signposting on the St Cuthbert's Way is
ridiculously good (symbol is a cross). Saw a few poeple on the route
today but very few. The morning weather was gloriously good but
then all afternoon it drizzled, which wet everything.

Have developed the habit of picking the fat off my pemmy
and just eating the meat fragments, leaving the fat to use as a fire
accelerant – a GREAT new innovation! I quite like the time and
effort that it takes (like the foraging exercises that they give animals
in Zoos to stop boredom, or perhaps smoking a pipe) – helps me
to relax and take stock rather than stress about how far I've got and
need to go.

Was going to push on till 5pm but stopped at 4 because really
shattered. A few times in the day I've hit the wall, but a stop and
some water and a morsel helped a great deal. The foraging has
extended to Jack-of-the-hedge (garlic mustard). The sorrel though
is food sent from God – lovely sharp off-set to fatty food, and quite
'meaty' itself. I'm always scanning the verges and hedgerows, and all
other margins; eyes down all the time.

The scenery today was really lovely, with freedom to walk through all of it from farmlands, watersides, woods and forests. Yesterday, on the way down from the Cheviots, it seemed as though the walkers were barred from the streams and rivers, with Deer fences all along the route, or else private land. Today it's been easy to get water and I'm pleased with my discipline with it – always keeping a full extra bottle for the evening. The woods I've just come through were beautiful, and I'm just looking for more of the Yew trees that were around earlier. They provide such gorgeous dry shelter underneath. There don't seem to be any now though. I'm on a ridge-top on Dere Street (old Roman Road, now a distinct track), and have skirted around a clump of gorse bushes to find a densely leafed ash with dry ground underneath – good. There are some large sycamore trees that are in leaf on the other side of the track, but some walkers have just gone past quite close, and anyway not sure there's enough leaf on them to give any shelter. Had wanted to make it to the next conifer forest but not sure that I could.

Made pemmy brew once settled in – MUCH more palatable. Fed fat to the stove – GREAT. Getting quite cold now. Everything a bit damp. Going to have some whisky and turn in.

Easter Bank Holiday Monday 17th April. Dere Street to Gala Hill, nr Galashiels. 'Beauty Spot Bivi'.

Morning

Not a very good night but at least stayed dry. Felt damp in sleeping bag – should have put silkies on. Menstrual blood this morning. GRIEF! Was thinking all last night what to send home when I get to Galashiels to lighten the load: sunblock, neutrogena hand cream, notebook, extra plastic bags are the obvious things. Don't want to just dump them.

Misty this morning – quite nice. Frightened by the distance/ time I have to go.

Evening

Left Bivi at 8a.m. Everything still a bit damp feeling. Today the weather has been good though varied: sun/light showers/cold/hot – mainly on the sunnier side. Getting VERY cold now though, at around 6p.m. Feels like another very long day. Dere St. was really lovely; gentle, tree-lined all the way. St Cuthbert's Way altogether very genteel.

Took a slight detour to avoid a meander in the river Tweed, but sorry I did so since Tweed exceptionally lovely. Melrose also good place. Stopped there to shed gear and have lunch of pemmy and sorrel. Had some nice chats about walking/ backpacking. Very popular up here. No wonder since the trails are so good.

The bleeding has been a nuisance. Hard work managing the blood. Completely unexpected as well. Have stopped pooing as well, which doesn't actually feel to be a problem but is a noticeable change.

My spirits lifted this morning when I saw a hazy mist with sun burning through. Put on quite a good pace. Quite a sharp hill though at the end of today, over Galashiels. On tired legs it took it out of me. Was really rewarding to get to the distinctive Eildon Hills today (remind me of some of the Shropshire hills like at Pontesbury). You can see them in the distance from the Cheviots, like a beacon, so get a sense of distance under my belt.

Very cold now. Feel my writing is a bit bland. It's all about getting the next thing done, and the next.

Stopped at 4pm and bivi set by 5. Children and parents are walking in sight of me and me of them. Some have remarked that there's a person camping in the woods – told to stay away, then father peering at my camp. He didn't realise he was looking straight at me so I gave a cheery hello and he explained that he was trying to make it out. Getting a bit quieter now. Going to light a fire and make hot pemmy. Don't want a smoking fire, so will need to heat it up with plenty of pemmy wrappers.

Night 2: 'Oak Tree Bivi', drying kit in the sunshine.

Night 1: 'Moonlight Bivi', at daybreak.

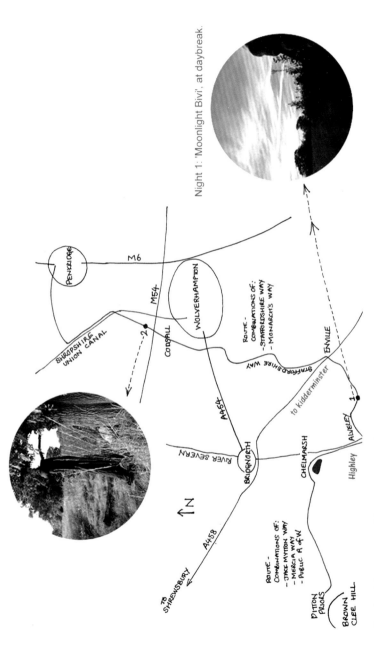

A sketch of the route and bivi sites on the 'Initiation Leg'.

'Sickness Leg', days Two and Three. The Staffordshire Way.

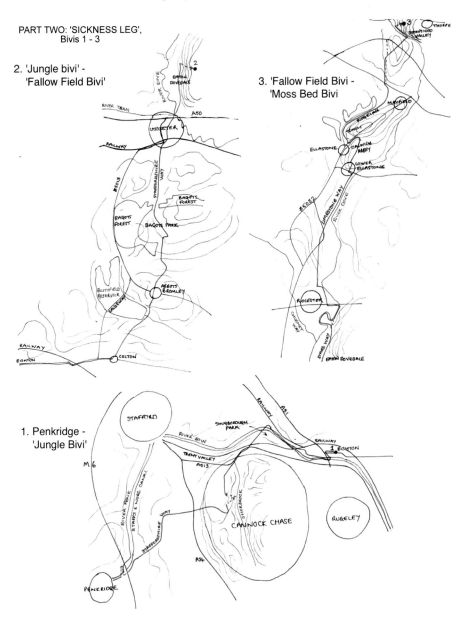

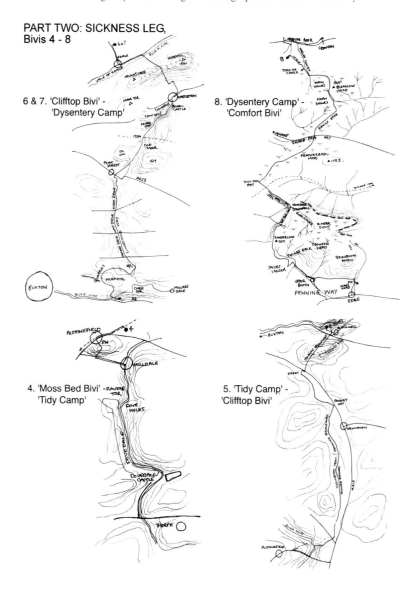

PART TWO: SICKNESS LEG,
Bivis 4 - 8

6 & 7. 'Clifftop Bivi' -
'Dysentery Camp'

8. 'Dysentery Camp' -
'Comfort Bivi'

4. 'Moss Bed Bivi' -
'Tidy Camp'

5. 'Tidy Camp' -
'Clifftop Bivi'

PART TWO: SICKNESS LEG, Bivis 9 - 12

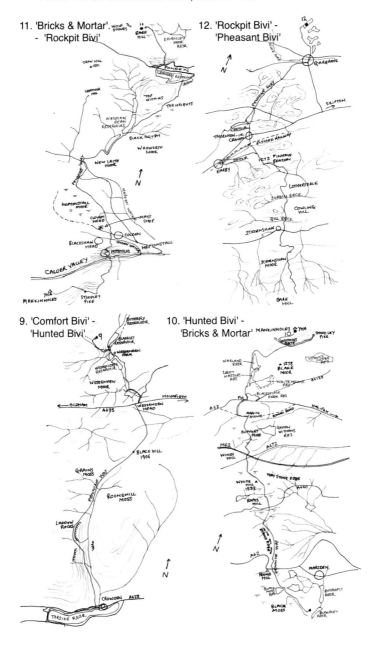

11. 'Bricks & Mortar' - 'Rockpit Bivi'

12. 'Rockpit Bivi' - 'Pheasant Bivi'

9. 'Comfort Bivi' - 'Hunted Bivi'

10. 'Hunted Bivi' - 'Bricks & Mortar'

'Sickness Leg', days Thirteen to Fifteen. Ending in the Yorkshire Dales.

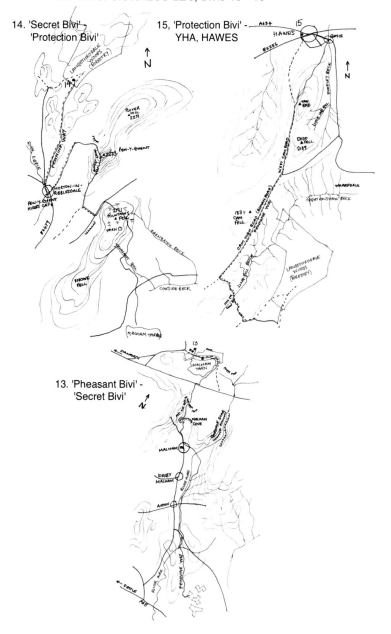

PART TWO: SICKNESS LEG, Bivis 13 - 15

14. 'Secret Bivi' - 'Protection Bivi'

15, 'Protection Bivi' - YHA, HAWES

13. 'Pheasant Bivi' - 'Secret Bivi'

'Bad Weather Leg', days One to Three. Coninuing on the Southern Pennines.

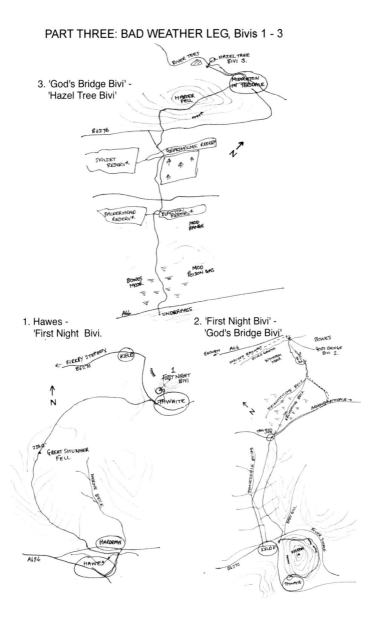

‘Bad Weather Leg’, days Four to Six. Touching Cumbria.

PART THREE: BAD WEATHER LEG, Bivis 4 - 6

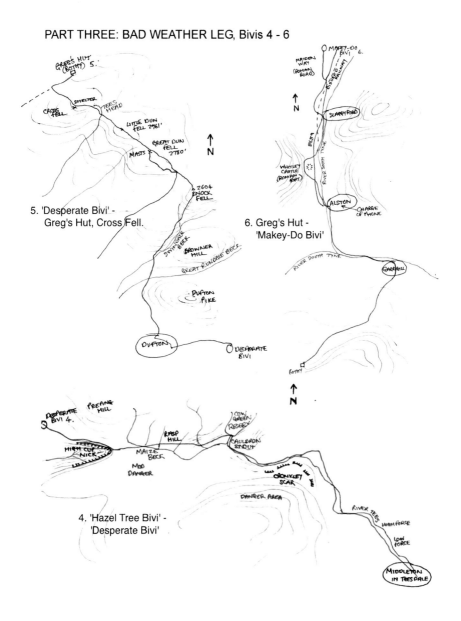

5. 'Desperate Bivi' -
Greg's Hut, Cross Fell.

6. Greg's Hut -
'Makey-Do Bivi'

4. 'Hazel Tree Bivi' -
'Desperate Bivi'

PART THREE: 'BAD WEATHER LEG', Bivis 7 - 9

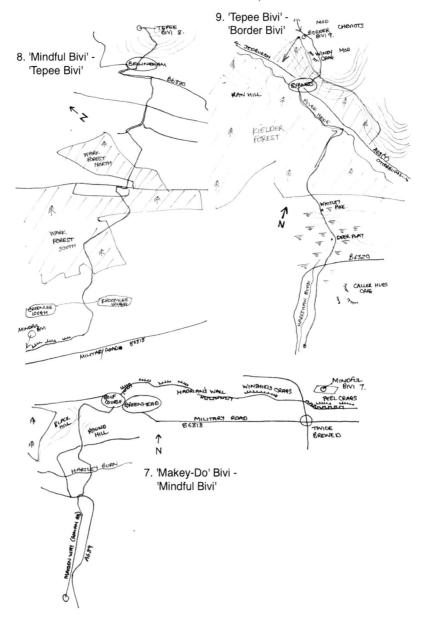

'Crazy Leg', days One and Two. Ending the Pennine Way.

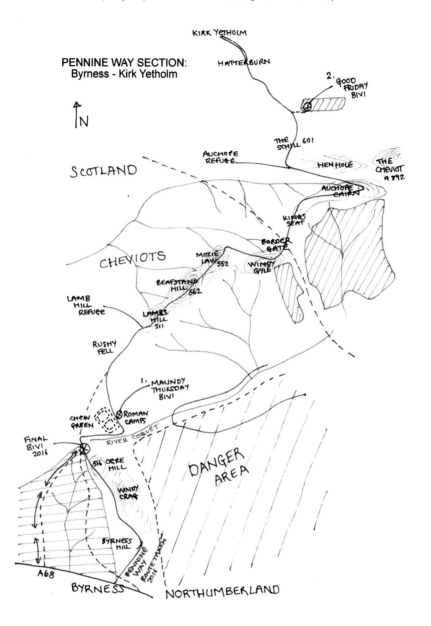

PENNINE WAY SECTION:
Byrness - Kirk Yetholm

KIRK YETHOLM

HATTERBURN

2. GOOD FRIDAY BIVI

N

THE SCHILL 601

SCOTLAND

AUCHOPE REFUGE

HEN HOLE

THE CHEVIOT 8 892

AUCHOPE CAIRN

KINGS SEAT

BORDER GATE

CHEVIOTS

MOZIE LAW 552

WINDY GYLE

BEAFSTAND HILL 662

LAMB HILL REFUGE

LAMBS HILL 511

RUSHY FELL

1. MAUNDY THURSDAY BIVI

CHEW GREEN

ROMAN CAMPS

FINAL BIVI 2016

RIVER COQUET

516 ORRE HILL

DANGER AREA

WINDY CRAG

BYRNESS HILL

PENNINE WAY ROUTE TAKEN 2016

A68

BYRNESS

NORTHUMBERLAND

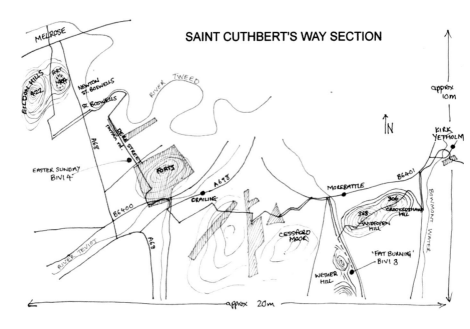

'Crazy Leg', days Three to Six. The St. Cuthbert's Way
and Southern Upland way sections.

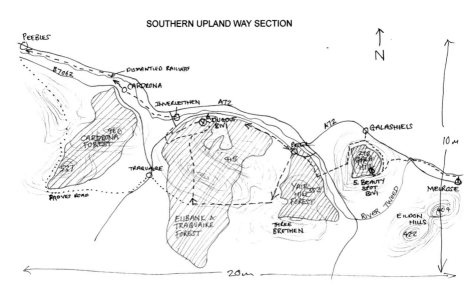

'Crazy Leg', days Seven and Eight. The Droves Road section, approaching Edinburgh.

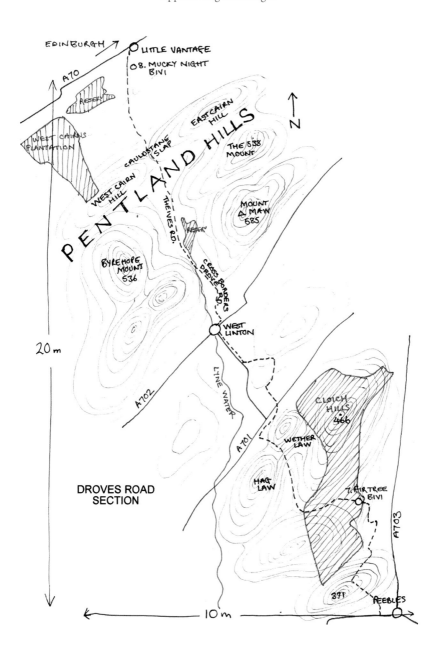

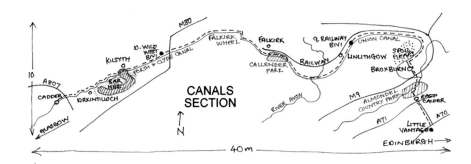

'Crazy Leg', days Nine and Ten, the Canals section.

'Crazy Leg', days Eleven to Seventeen. The West Highland Way section.

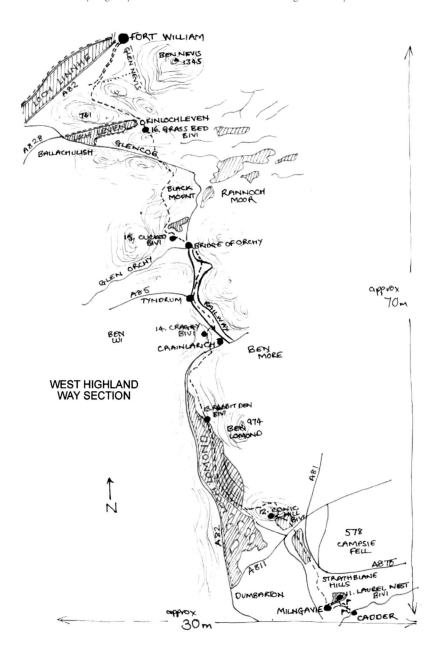

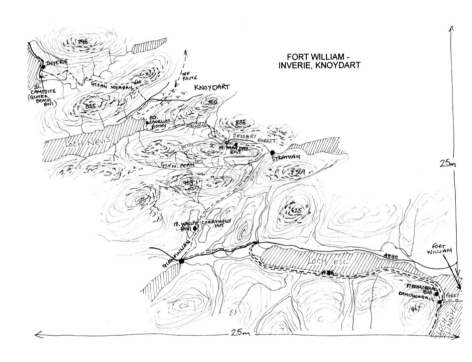

'Crazy Leg', days Eighteen to Twenty-One. The Final section from Fort William to Knoydart.

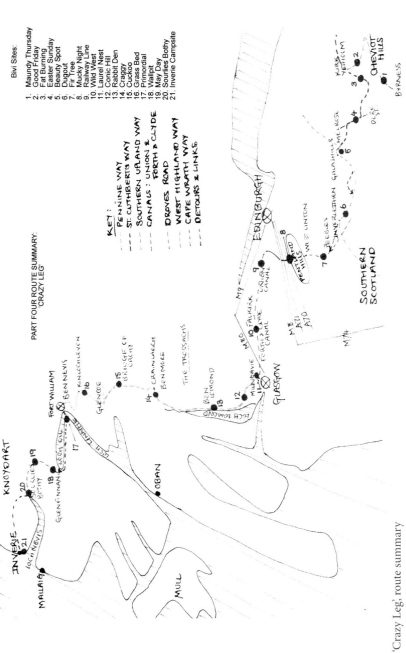

Bivi Sites:

1. Maundy Thursday
2. Good Friday
3. Fat Burning
4. Easter Sunday
5. Beauty Spot
6. Dugout
7. Fir Tree
8. Mucky Night
9. Railway Line
10. Wild West
11. Laurel Nest
12. Conic Hill
13. Rabbit Den
14. Craggy
15. Cuckoo
16. Grass Bed
17. Primordial
18. Wallpit
19. May Day
20. Sourlies Bothy
21. Inverie Campsite

PART FOUR ROUTE SUMMARY:
'CRAZY LEG'

KEY:
— PENNINE WAY
— — ST. CUTHBERT'S WAY
— — SOUTHERN UPLAND WAY
— — CANALS : UNION &
       FORTH & CLYDE
— — DROVES ROAD
— — WEST HIGHLAND WAY
— — CAPE WRATH WAY
— — DETOURS & LINKS

'Crazy Leg', route summary

Sketch map of entire route for the Expedition

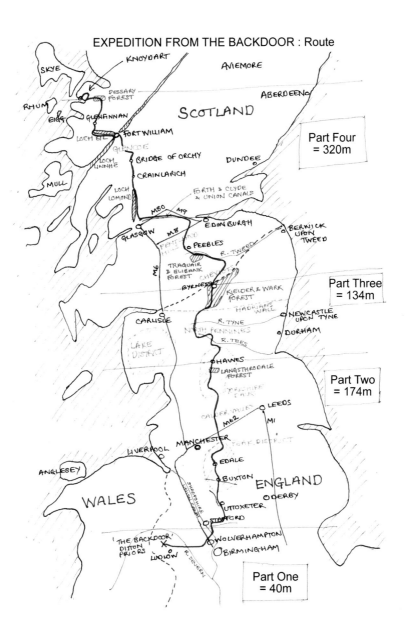

EXPEDITION FROM THE BACKDOOR : Route

Provisions of sauerkraut, pemmican portions and dates for the 'Sickness Leg'.

Kit for the 'Sickness Leg', with added cat!

Weather-worn on Pen-y-Ghent, Yorkshire Dales.

'Great Shunner', the first day on 'Bad Weather Leg'.

Making-do on 'Bad Weather Leg'.

Cooking up some pemmican at 'Dugout Bivi', 'Crazy Leg'.

The basha makes a shelter on 'Mucky Night Bivi', 'Crazy Leg'.

Cooking kit of: tinder, knife, striker, and tin-can stove.

Listening to the wind, 'Crazy Leg'.

Second day of 'Crazy Leg', on the Cheviots.

Thistle roots, sorrel and bittercress to eat.

A portion of pemmican with sorrel leaves.

Shelter on 'Bad Weather Leg'. Northumberland.

Arcoss Rannoch Moor, 'Crazy Leg'.

Checking the route after the West Highland Way.

The River Tees, 'Bad Weather Leg'.

Reaching Inverie, Knoydart.

Suffering feet on 'Bad Weather Leg'.

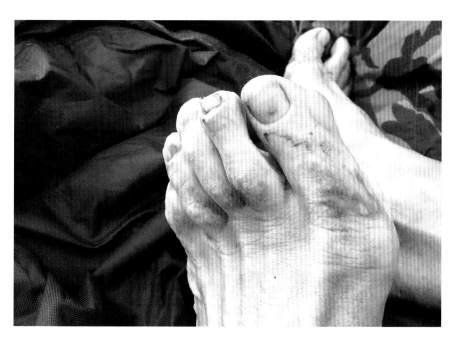

The diary, made from route maps.

I find that as soon as I've set up a bivi I get a territorial sense about it, so I don't feel apologetic or embarrassed to be there. If anything I would challenge intruders about THEIR rights and intentions in coming close. I think it's partly because I've worked so hard to get there and in fact need to make camp. It straightens out the priorities for me.

Today have gained the Southern Upland Way – JOY!

Tuesday 18th April. Galashiels to Elibank and Traquair Forest. 'Dugout Bivi'

Morning

Gained the Southern Upland Way at Melrose and continued on towards Galashiels yesterday. Stopped at 4pm and set up 'Beauty Spot' bivi, in woods on top of steep hill. Another public location, where my camp has been remarked upon and stared at and a magnet for dogs.

Had a good night – comfort – but wakeful after midnight worrying about whether if I continue to take the Southern Upland Way it will take too long. Also worrying about the John Muir's way on the canals and how I'll cope. Man I met yesterday said I'll have to take my chances for a bivi on the canals (backpacker himself, but mainly bike touring I think).

Frost this a.m. And red sky! Beautiful day so far. Have decided to throw away things rather than go into Galashiels to post them home: some pemmican (have allowed for a portion/day since that's what I seem to get through, but chucking some feels like Shackleton killing the dogs), bandage, lead shot from survival kit (fishing weights), handcream, sunblock, deodorant, extra charging cable mistakenly brought, four heavy weight A4 size plastic bags, instant coffee (which I found disgusting when I tried. Wanted to make dandelion coffee but takes an age to get roots up and dry them). The bundle feels reasonably heavy, so might gain by getting rid.

Lots of passers-by last night. Red setter wouldn't go back to annoyed owner – liked the smell of pemmy too much.

Mid morning

This morning woke at 5.30am, left about 7 to have breakfast in sunlight. Finally set off at 7.30. Galashiels – dumped stuff in bin. Find myself counting miles and hours – not so good always under pressure of time. On hard terrain doing about 2.5m per hour. Thought I saw a dog on opposite hillside following along behind a tractor. Turned out to be a calf being led back to its mother. Good mix of livestock around here.

Thoroughly enjoyed first bit of Southern Upland Way section, but at meeting river Tweed hip hurt v. badly and clunking/scraping bones. Decided that foolish to push my legs over the hills all day when I have no rest days planned. Decided to walk along the river (exceptional) to Inverleithen. Washed my 'smalls' in river to dry in sun on my pack.

Walked initially with two local men: Stuart (a keen walker, who used to work for the gas company and laid the gas pipes along the route. He showed us the markers), his friend (didn't catch his name) who is having chemotherapy at the moment and is being helped to develop his hillwalking skills/motivation by Stuart.

Sunny day and at times very hot, interspersed with cold wind and cloud. Wouldn't want it any hotter. Thought I heard some kind of industrial plant in the valley – turned out to be a sit-on lawn mower!

Got into a good pattern now with Kit and food. Hazelnuts and prunes for breakfast (not very tasty, prunes not very sweet and nuts very hard – STOPS ME SCOFFING!) and spoonful of sauerkraut (the salt is like a boost in the morning – like taking coffee), sauerkraut and pemmy for lunch, heated and partially rehydrated pemmy for dinner, sip of whisky at bed.

People I'm meeting are very calm(ing) and pleasant/ straightforward. I'm very partial to the accent.

Afternoon

When I reached Peel my hip was much better, so I decided to regain the hills (big additional mileage). By the time I got to Elibank and Traquair forest, was absolutely wasted. Rain threatened so took track down into forest to try and work out what to do next. Religious about staying dry at the end of the day. Must stop and take stock. Must have done over 20m today. Now 5pm.

Evening

Feeling a bit hopeless tonight so I'm having to do some more writing and taking a swig of whisky. I'm in forestry woods – proper – feeling a bit scary really on account of the strange, tall deadness of it. The green stuff is all very high up. I've found a fallen tree stump to string my basha across that gives me a spot of level ground (a pit where the roots were dragged up when the tree fell over. Otherwise VERY steep hillside. It's an earth pit essentially – 'Dugout Bivi'. Feels weird. There's wood sorrel growing on the sides that softens the earthiness.

In truth I feel a bit tearful. It's been a long slog today and I've been torn about route choices. Silly really. It's whether to go over the esoteric routes of Hamish Brown, or use the Drovers road over the hills, or stick to paths in the valleys. Indecision today led to both. Trouble with the first option is spending the whole day route-finding and stuffing my chances of getting to Inverie, trouble with second is (possibly) knackering terrain, but the third will probably sap my morale. I'll have to let myself stew on it tonight.

Walking here to my bivi met a man with a dog. BAD. He was really hostile, staring me down when I nodded a greeting. Made me feel vulnerable. That's probably why the woods feel scary tonight. It's why I've climbed onto such a steep slope looking down on the track. Makes me worry about later on the walk.

Lots of midges here but not biting. Soil is sandy so not making kit dirty – just as well in a pit in the ground

Wednesday 19th April. Dugout Bivi, nr Inverleithen to Kilnubie Hill.

'Fir Tree Bivi.'

Morning

Church bells softly peeling this morning woke me gently – first at 3 and then at 5. Good rest. Not so cold in the night. Tongue feels VERY dry and a bit swollen. Mouth open all night perhaps because nose blocked. Combed hair this morning and looked at self. Much wind burn. Now have a hydrocolloid plaster on each ankle where the boots rub. The pack is a bit awkward too because I need it above my hips to be comfortable and the straps keep slipping loose. Tied knots in them, but means I have to keep untying them to get the pack back on, then tie them again. Taking my pills for the day in one fell swoop in the morning rather than splitting between morning and night so I don't forget to take them.

Took the forest tracks out this morning. MTB (bike) runs all over the hillside. Each route description was 'extreme', with 'mandatory air' – decided after thinking about it not to take any of these down incase of (unlikely) cyclist at 7.30am. Wondered where the 'nursery' routes were. All routes had boards with emergency info. and escape routes indicated. Eventually found 'Matador' – an ascent and descent route, so figured okay. Reached Inverliethen.

Decided that after such a long day yesterday and no chance of any rest days I'd take dismantled railway route to Peebles. Was expecting it to be nice and ramshackle alongside the Tweed, but Tarmac all the way, signage, and not much view of the river. Traffic sound from 'A' road quite loud. Still – direct route so thankful for that. Route goes through Cardona Village, which turned out to be through a housing estate rather than the village. Strange estate. Houses all looked quite solid done in stone (clad probably) to come across as traditional, but unmistakably new. Pristine place. Lines of blue-topped bins along the street. Immaculate. Only one piece of litter – a till receipt. Posh but not very edifying. Looked like made of building blocks. When got back to the railway looked as though could have just skirted the golf course. Obviously unwanted on the links.

Evening

Stopped at 4.30 on the Droves Road that goes over the border (over the Pentland Hills). Had a clear sky when got to Cloich Hills Forest to bivi, so thought I might be in for a cold night, but cloud cover has built. Now 7.30. Bivi is underneath fir tree 'Fir Tree Bivi' in a little dip, so couldn't light a fire there and had to find alternative site to cook. All finished now. Put mish-mash in pot, a la 'pong' (the cook) of Rum Doodle[28]. Tasted good enough.

Peebles quite picturesque (apart from caravan/holiday park on way out on Drovers road). Did a bit more washing in stream (especially hands which are black from soot that's been worked into them with the pemmy grease).

First poo since weekend – a relief! Body getting into gear now.

Met many people whilst having lunch on riverside bench in Peebles. Dogs continue to gravitate. Looked like rain and v.cold wind so put on appropriate gear, but dissipated suddenly to clear

---

28 'The Ascent of Rum Doodle' by Bowman.

warm skies. Did the same thing again later. Now on the Drover's Road towards the big smoke (outskirts of Edinburgh).

Late

Sent a picture home to help Andy with the blog posts. Feels wrong. He messaged me that there's to be a general election in June, but don't want to think about all that now. My strength seems to be growing, and not so much pain in hip – but don't want to jinx it. Learning that doing things the bushcraft way you have to take it really slowly. Like lighting a fire and organising kit – as well as stopping to deal with the small things that might turn into big things. It's the antithesis of contemporary life, especially the sports I've been involved with. Even in Alpinism speed is key to safety – getting off the mountain by early afternoon. I'm having to pace myself and stop trying to outrun the rain clouds – just make sure everything is protected for when they let rip. In fact, when I'm on the hills I don't much mind about keeping to plan – like 16m/day come hell or high water. Only at night get bothered. It's a very long way with almost 20kg over series of steep hills, especially in bad weather, so what can I do except just make the best plans?

Feeling much happier than yesterday. Beginning to rely on evening ration of cooked pemmy – very nourishing. Everywhere around the bivi site is sodden, because I'm in a clearing with only a few saplings, except under this bigger (but rather cute) fir, which is bone dry. I'm doing without the tarp/basha since foliage cover is dense. WE SHALL SEE!

Just thinking about today and recalling coming across main roads to Glasgow and Edinburgh in Peebles. Gave me a thrill! BUT bloody nav in towns got me again – still hopeless.

Thursday 20th April. Fir Tree Bivi to A70, nr Little Vantage. Mucky Night Bivi

Morning

Was a very still night – only occasionally the very slightest wisp of coldness across the face. First mozzies, first use of mozzi repellent. 4.40 am now and plane just gone across – Edinburgh? Been awake for a long time thinking about route plans. Had DREAMS in night. Woke up laughing in middle of night. Not had that for years and years. Dream that was training for boxing but didn't want hernias in my arms?? Two other dreams that I was desperate to remember but now they've gone – so must have been important! Wonder whether some delirium is setting in ? Fasting visions?

Very comfortable night. A lot of T-Witting from a solitary owl, eventually got a T-woo from a distance then left. Also something came to visit early am but didn't see what it was.

10.40am

Have hiked over to West Linton. Was wondering on the way, through the forested hillside, why I do this. Asking myself the question like an interview. I thought, and he probably doesn't know and wouldn't approve (from concern) that my father in law (and my husband Andy) are big inspiration – the Primroses, hailing from around here. Then there's my mother and her grandfather, the MacIntoshes, Hailing from the Highlands. Made me ponder, Highland/Lowland, West and East, Yin and Yang. I like the thought of all this just coming from feeling touched by history.

After silent forest walk and hillsides and burns the last stretch to West Linton was 1.5 miles on the road. NOT NICE. I noticed, after several incidents of the same, how when girls and women all past me they smell overpoweringly of perfume. It makes me wonder what makes them think they smell so bad that they have to do this – put on chemicals. Not exactly a rhetorical question! It makes me think, with all this pemmican on me and in me that I must smell, like the wife in 'A Whole Life' by Seethaler, vaguely 'meaty'. Dog's delight!

Having a long stop here before heading out over the Pentlands. Unusual place. Refuge of the last Covenanters apparently[29]. Thinking I'll probably have to camp out on the hillside tonight coz a long, woodless tract on the Droves road and Thieves road. Started this am at 7.00am and stopped now at 10.40. That's long enough for a decent break.

Evening

Loved the Pentlands. Pooped now though due to interminable path around bogs coming down. Had my eye on a forest the other side of a sheep field just below A70 but wanted to stop now, so have just set up bivi on sheltered side of field wall leading up to the road. Been v.v. windy. Couldn't easily manage my body temp and felt a bit sick. Was thrilled when the Forth bridges came into view – feels like a milestone. Bivi is in a lush field with muck spread all over it. Quite dry though and not smelling – I think! Used one of plastic gloves in med kit to clear the area. Can hear gulls

Friday 21st April. A70 to Railway Line Bivi, the Union Canal, east of Linlithgow.

Morning

6am now. Red sunrise! Got virtually no sleep. Wondering about physical

---

29   Scottish Presbyterians who bound themselves, through covenants, to maintaining their doctrine as the only religion in Scotland.

health and whether another two weeks on rations is possible – esp. with blood in urine. But it IS though, isn't it? What about Shackeltons crew? Although I don't have the luxury of penguins to eat! Rain and wind ALL night, but sheltered from effects if not sounds. Quite warm. Tarp performed superbly – better than poncho used to. Having to remind myself to be meticulous about sanitising hands in this field – don't want e-coli from the grass. 'Mucky Night Bivi'! Dry mouth ALL the time – I think mainly from breathing through mouth.

Will have to pack everything up in very confined quarters today – luxury of space is over – so as to stay dry. In the night had to cool myself down rapidly due to feeling sick. Far too many coverings in this warm wet weather. Wonder how walking will be now. I had wished for rain along the canals to keep everyone off them. May rue the thought!

Odd noises overnight were very strange – industrial, whining and deep, inhuman kind of gearing sort of sounds. I'm right by the A70, Forth Bridges, wind turbines, flight paths – so whether one or other or all responsible don't know.

Leaving at 7.30. Rain has stopped and some sunshine, but dark clouds too.

Evening

Been a mixed day but I'm feeling quite fresh still – must be the flat walking (canal-side). From the Almondel Park (rather grander than what I took from the 'delightful' credited by JPButler). I decided to head due North to pick up the Union canal rather than pick it up earlier and head East then West again on the towpath. However, though started well on lovely country road (with foraging) it soon became hellish with traffic – and Broxburn lifts the spirits not one bit! I got back on the canal round the spoil heaps (quite interesting/appealing to me) and found it not dull at all. Going under bridges hit by gusts of wind that nearly knocked me off balance.

Work being done on the towpath all way to Linlithgow, meaning a few tight dances around surfacing machinery. Very friendly workmen. Couple on tandem – much taller one in front (the man) going hell for leather shouted back at me "well packed up" which pleases me – one of my standards met! Enjoyed walking along canal. Been told it would be very boring – maybe it will become so, but for now nice to have the changed scenery and not to be going up and down all day. Thankfully, have now fixed the rubbing of the boots on my ankles by moving the leather between the tongues of each boot in the opposite direction. The leather is so soft its quite cooperative. Have also developed a routine with the pack straps that is working okay, but not wholly solved that one.

Thought I might walk later into the evening and take my chances on bivi, but saw a suitable field, next to a railway line 'Railway Bivi' which is always good in terms of privacy – just outside Lilithgow. Was told it would be hard to wild camp on the canal – maybe it will get so.

Later pm

I'm trying to remember all my bivi sites but I'm having a job to do it. Most have been in forests but I'm diversifying now – a wallside in a field yesterday and a field by a railway and canal today. I had to write some more because a gent came towards me walking his dog – wolfhound – and was quite surprised and embarrassed saying he hadn't seen me. I smiled and said "good. That's the idea". However he went on to apologise and say that he wanted to give Alfie a run off the track. I had geared myself up for him to be the farmer or someone living nearby wanting to clear me off, not as someone who thought I had more right to be here than him.

Can hear an ice cream van.

I've had my pemmican and whisky. It's not getting any more palatable but I MAKE myself eat it (like altitude training) so that I can get to Inverie at all. In the day often feel myself weaken through hunger, so I need to keep my condition up. Threw away 4 more portions of pemmy today having worked out I didn't need them – they're very heavy. Been collecting firewood along the way each day for the evening. Today some trouble lighting but got it going eventually. Having an early night (7.30) coz had so little sleep last night. Clear skies so far. Going to get cold? Spirits are a little higher now. Worked out I need to do 15m/day all the way through, but I'm going to try and put in more on the canal stretch to give me leeway later. Funnily I haven't seen the West Highland Way (WHW for short) as looming so large as the other sections have done. I think because I was concerned about bivis on the canals, and expect my pack to be lighter for the WHW. I might be being a bit blind to the difficulties ahead. Feel as though I'm getting fitter now though.

Saturday 22nd April. Linlithgow to Authincioch, Forth and Clyde Canal. Wild West Bivi

Morning

5am. Beautiful night. Stars. Mild. Calling of one of those birds from early hours that sound a bit like a vibrating spring. Bit alarming last night when different kind of rumble (not trains or cars) started up and got closer and closer. Looked out and saw a tractor spreading on my field and coming towards me in the dusk. I thought "shit" – literally! Muck spreading. It would be all over for me if he was as avid as the farmer from last night's field since he'd managed to get it up the walls and over the path on the other side – even on the information boards about Cauldstane Slap (on the Pentlands above). But he seemed (kindly) to give me a bit of space and what he was spreading didn't smell. I watched him going up and down till fell asleep.

Woke and the sky was dotted with bright stars. Wished I wasn't under the basha so I could look straight up at it. More dreams last night of peculiar kinds. Varied dawn chorus as I write – headtorch on to be able to see the page. Feeling quite cozy. Should get to (and beyond) Falkirk today (Primrose clan home). Will send picture back... maybe

Pee last night still bloody, but other bleeding stopped now.

Find myself resisting all meals now and having to force myself to have the sauerkraut and pemmican.

Lunchtime

Must have done about 12 miles this morning. Reached the Falkirk Wheel – thronging with people. Impressive (overengineered?!) thing just to link two small canals (Union and Forth and Clyde). I'm pooped now and having a good rest. Took my first fall this morning, bending down for some bittercress in walls of the Falkirk Tunnel with pack on. Luckily fall on my back not such an issue with such a bulky pack on. Had a few good chats with people again. Of course its Sat hols so a lot of folk on the canal, especially cyclists (some nice, some not). The Avon aqueduct on the Union canal is gorgeous. Managed to get down to the river Avon for fresh water – took the climb back up very slowly though.

Now starting to worry about the West Highland Way, especially since Andy messaged that wintery weather on the way. It looks as though it will be over by the time I get to the end of WHW at Fort William. I wonder how busy the trail will be in the bad weather. At the moment the sun is really hot but an icy wind, so when it clouds over (all the time) it gets freezing. NOT GOOD FOR MY REYNAULDS. Must eat some pemmy now. Oh – and talk of wild camping being impossible or difficult on the canal just seems wrong – unless the Forth-Clyde is very different from the Union.

Another breakage (now fixed) – the elastic snapped on the

raincover for the pack so I had to re-thread it this morning on route. Thankfully wasn't raining.

Evening

Keep forgetting what day it is and have to keep counting and recounting. Pretty sure its Saturday and that I have two weeks left, but keep having a fright and thinking only one week left. It was a long slog from the outskirts of Falkirk to the wheel, and all the time I was just assuming that that's where I needed to get to. The map wasn't clear on routes onto the canals. Then I came across a bike route sign for the John Muir Way that pointed off the canal saying 24hr access to the Forth and Clyde – made me worry that I'd go all that way blindly following the sign for the wheel and have to come back. As it turned out there was a footbridge at the wheel that gets closed at 8pm. Sometimes you need to do just a bit of research!

Lots of cyclists on the path, a group doing John Muir spoke to me. Some walkers also inquired what I was up to. Mixed bag in terms of encounters. One stone-faced bloke crossed my path on the Forth & Clyde canal just as I was looking for a bivi pitch. I've been going from 6.30am to 5pm with 45min lunch and ready to stop now.

Saw my first bluebells of season at Falkirk. Also managed to forage sorrel, bittercress, fiddleheads (bracken tops), gorse flowers. Carrying some larch needles as well saved from forest – very soft and fragrant, tangy taste (no tannin yet). Have set up on a lovely looking stretch where the canal opens up and starts to look like a river. Busy though, as well as houses and roads in view. I'm in a silver birch and hawthorn copse which is hard to penetrate. There's a well used deer track through it.

About 18/19m today – but it's not how far you've come, it's how far there is to go!

Sunday 23rd April. Wild West Bivi to woods nr Baldernock, Milngavie: 'Laurel Nest Bivi'

Morning

Keep talking to myself in an Irish accent. This morning heard coming out of my mouth "sure glad that dream's over Ted" as Dougal from Father Ted. Also "she can't show it but she's in pain" as Noel the Supervet when he puts his hand on yet another 'victim's' knee until they cry (until of course he tells them he can help) – we love him. Actually I'm getting quite hallucinatory now – hearing people talking as I walk, usually from the natural noises around me. The birdsongs become pertinent phrases (usually encouraging ones), and my constant di-dumming musical phrase accompanying each step goes on in my head all the time – even when I'm lying down.

Its 5.30am now. Last night dogs started yapping excitedly and I couldnt tell where they were. They went on for hours and I wondered if they were from the house opposite and were disturbed by me. I'd put up a screen from my pack liner in the evening to stop myself looking straight at their house. Also noticed a little stream that is not fed by the canal that I might try to get to for some water. People were walking their dogs all evening on the towpath. Cars all night on adjacent road. VERY PUBLIC. A lot of shooting somewhere. Gent training spaniel to fetch quarry quite near to me on riverbank.

Just heard thundering sound then saw lovely thing – about a dozen horses galloping around their field. Appaloosa horses. White freckled rumps. Watching them for ages. Wild West Bivi!

Lunchtime

It's 1.30pm. I'm now at Cadder, above Glasgow, sitting in the sun but covering up every few minutes from icy blasts (quite

Apline feeling). This is where I leave the canals. I quite enjoyed them – lots of variety in fact. Not a bit the urban waterways I had in my imagination (Wolverhampton and Reading are the ones I know).

Saw several deer making their way through my copse this morning. I'm on North of Glasgow now, but wouldn't know it one bit. Met a lot of people this am who stopped to chat. One man (and his wife) who is doing WHW with his son in a few weeks, but couldnt persuade his wife. He looked very outdoorsy. Very differently met a woman on a bike (fraid my reactions are mean and a bit judgmental). She had all the biking gear on. Has done lots in Scotland (incl. WHW). Said off walking in Pyrenees this year and saving for Appalachian trail. Can't fault her for wanting to, but she gave me too much unsolicited advice, including to take bananas and water on one of the sections because it is "completely unsupported". That's the problem isn't it? Whats wrong with water on the hill? I'm sure its not a desert! She told me where it is hardest on the knees and to take time and enjoy Loch Lomond, so now have it in my head that it gets bloody after that!

Foraged some lovely sweet vetch and some nettles. Actually looking forward to my meals now. Maybe getting through the nuts and prunes a bit fast.

One way that it seems very scottish here is the regimen on the towpath. I like to walk on the right but have given up because everyone seems to comply with the roads and cling to the left. No anarchy here then! Expecting crowds of walkers and big send-off at Milngavie for the WHW by all accounts!!!

Very pleased that this am pee was proper shade and quantity. Menstrual bleeding fully stopped now – thank goodness that hassle is over. Collected some reed mace heads for firelighting just now (before leaving the canals).

Evening

Butler's route off the canal and to Milngavie is really lovely, once you have mustered the 'face' to see it through on the second golf course (v private). The first one was easy – had a public path running through with signage. Easy. But nothing helpful on the second. Had to just make for little stream and try to follow it. Players were helpful though when stream became inaccessible. Between the golf courses (on the way to Balmore) I foraged some lesser celandine tubers (tiny but abundant) to add to the pot. Followed a dog sauntering ahead of me towards second golf course – turned out to be a large and very confident fox.

When left the second golf course at Fluchter an older couple got chatting to me about where I was going/come from. Got help from the man about best way to Milngavie. It was the one I'd intended to take. They used to walk a lot they told me. The woman liked independent walkers (and demonstrated by walking off ahead of her husband!!) and he used to cycle all around this area when younger. On holiday here.

Great views over towards Glasgow.

I went on my way and met Alan, a Glaswegian, out walking, pole in hand – related discussion about dog attacks – and Hitech boots (cheap but for him better coz not narrow like boots made on the continent – here here!). After describing my expedition he said he was proud of me, which made me feel very good. At first I witheld where he might find me online, but decided to give him Farafoot web address coz he was so supportive and friendly to me. He said he would love to do what I'm doing but scared of getting wet since can't get things dry. My biggest worry too. Been religious about keeping myself dry – putting on goretex as soon as hints of rain and keeping bedding dry. Luckily my bivi bag doesn't seem to be prone to condensation inside so that's a big help. Took Alan a week to do WHW so must ensure put in the miles when I can.

I've set up bivi near a ford in the road in what looks like public park woodland. I'm on a little knoll in a nest of laurel 'Laurel Nest Bivi'. Have strung tarp to the tree so I can quickly peg it out if rain, but won't bother unless need to. Feeling not too tired (not fit to drop tired), but stopped coz want to have a look at the WHW section route and get myself ready. Anxious. Now nearly 6pm. Will have a look at maps then sort out food.

Oh – there is a big building quite close making a lot of noise. Can't work out if industrial or amenity. Also Glasgow airport flightpath – don't mind that a bit

Monday 24th April. Laurel Nest Bivi to Conic Hill Bivi

Morning

Now 5.15 am. Basha is quite funny. Waterproof so far, it's just that I can have plans to string it out in a particular way but it just does what it wants and I have to make it up as I go along. I ended up with quite a bizarre thing last night (started to rain as soon as I began cooking so had to stop and sort it out).

Not only on flight path but must be very close to airport coz into late hours planes very low coming over. The nature of the building making the noise became clearer when I heard tennis being played. Someone's labrador came to visit and wouldn't leave, but at last picked up his ball and went when his owner called from afar.

Lunchtime

Was out walking with the first plane at 6.30. Started on West Highland Way at 7.30. Two lads there with camo packs. Well built. Bit macho? Some grunted hellos then they marched past. I felt really strongly that wanted to push ahead but talked to myself and kept it slow and steady. Meanly thinking they'll blow up anyhow. So competitive!

Very strong winds and gusts nearly blowing me over. Taking my breath. Had first hail shower and now another one during lunch break. Stopped at 11ish to harvest celandine tubers (lots and lots of them here). Getting very low on all but pemmican, so I'm going to need to get more than leaves. Will try for thistle and burdock if can find any. Sticks (walking poles) are getting MUCH shorter. Sad really, and quite dangerous because my 'trident' is now at face height! Maybe put ferrules on when back at home to stop more wearing down. Done 12.5miles on WHW and 1.5miles to Milngavie this am. Thinking of trying for Loch Lomond this pm. About 6miles over the tops. Did some washing in the stream – now drying in the wind. I find that even when I stop and forage etc. still get to my expected spot/expected time the same. Must just freshen me up.

Evening

Done 17miles. Was quite fresh when I stopped at about 4pm, but after faffing about with basha I'm quite knackered now. This spot under Conic Hill was lovely and shaded from the horrendous wind when I chose it, but must have changed direction coz now the basha is flapping like a sail. Talking of sails, my rain cover for pack was also catching the strong headwind all day and only stopped dragging me backwards when it kept ripping off! I've rigged clips on the top and bottom. Seem to work. Hoping the wind is going to drop tonight or I'm going to be worrying about the basha. If I take it down though, sure to rain. The headwind must be slowing me down as well – although not too worried about my effort today.

Will have to eat the fat from the pemmican tonight – all of it in the stew – so I don't fall over tomorrow, especially if we are getting more of the wintry blast. I've noticed that if I get inspired (by scenery) I walk better (stronger) even if the going is harder.

Had a good dinner. Thought I heard children playing but it was gulls squabbling.

FORAGED:
GREENS: beech leaves, nettles, fiddlehead, sorrel, larch needles, vetch
ROOTS/TUBERS: lesser celandine
Burned my tongue tonight. Too eager. Lovely lemony flavour from the larch.
Wind dropped during dinner but seems to be getting up again.

Tuesday 25th April. Conic Hill Bivi to Cailness, Loch Lomond. 'Rabbit Den Bivi'

Morning

Cold, windy night. I LOVE MY CACOON (sleeping bag liner). Put my phone charger and phone in bed with me to stop them freezing. Hare visited last night but didn't seem to notice me. Thought I heard something/ someone breathing or snoring all night. Just remembered as cleaning teeth that on the canals and before, but especially there, everyone smelled absolutely horrid. At first I thought it was just a few female runners (perfumes) but it was all the men as well. Clothes wash/ deodorisers? Really nauseating and lingered on and on.

Evening

Just set up bivi on slopes above Loch Lomond, under a yew tree – pillow is a rabbit den, hope they won't mind too much. Rabbit Den Bivi.

Can feel myself going down a bit. Takes me a long time to set bivi. Pooped but think I only did about 13miles today. I expected relatively flat since follows loch closely, but it is punishing ups and downs all the way. I feel hungry too. Back in Milngavie I tellingly paused a bit too long looking at the food bank! I've foraged some decent thistle roots today but it took time, and drew attention.

This bivi is far from ideal – not very sheltered – but I didn't know what I'd get if I carried on.

Can hear trains and cars on the other side of the loch it is so close. I suppose today did start with a hard climb in the headwind. On Conic Hill the wind was so bad I could hardly move. It was sunny all day with blasts of arctic wind. There was ice on the hill. The wind has been pushing against me all the way – tiring legs and head. On this terrain have to concentrate hard all day. Wind might drop overnight – seems to. Should be headed towards Crainlarich tomorrow.

Just had my stew – with sun setting over Loch Lomond and weather coming in from the north. Huddled over my stove. Now getting warmth from the embers as I write. Found myself a bone as a digging stick, though I have enough foraged stock for tomorrow so I won't have to stop. FREEZING NOW. GET IN SACK.

Wednesday 26th April. Loch Lomond to Crainlarich. 'Craggy Bivi'

Morning

5.13am. Just woken. Wind dropped last night. Felt warmer. Lights flickered on the basha from the road on the other side of the loch. At first thought it was someone out there deliberately being silent. Worried. Then realised light faster than sound which is why didn't correlate with cars exactly. Settled. At first couldn't sleep, then shifted and slept very soundly. Woke with father-in-law's comment "life is anabasis old chum".

Yesterday more perfumed/smelly people on the trail. Most, luckily, were alone and wanted it that way, or in pairs/groups and wanted it that way – good thing. I'M STILL UNSOCIABLE.

My clothes and hair smell of woodsmoke now.

MORNING ROUTINE:

1. Take trousers and socks from stash bag (my pillow) and put them in sleeping bag to warm.
2. Take down jacket and hat from pillow and put on.
3. Clean teeth and take meds.
4. Put on trousers and socks.
5. Get out of bed and put on boots.
6. Have a pee and attend to ablutions.
7. If weather dry take down basha.
8. Swap down jacket for primaloft jacket and goretex jacket.
9. Stuff clothes in bottom of pack, then med/bits bag, then sleeping bag and cacoon, then bivi bag, then pemmican and sauerkraut bags, then pillow sack containing mat, pegs, paracord and basha.
10. Collect firewood and put in stove bag.
11. Put cooking pots and stove in lid of pack.
12. Put whisky in side pocket.
13. Put day's food ration and foraging bag in pack belt pockets.
14. Put water, phone, maps, pen, knife, head torch, compass, whistle, glasses in bumbag.
15. Raincover on pack.

READY TO GO.

Just got out of bed and 6am. 'Alpenglow' on hills over other side of water – too brief for me to take picture. As I walk each day I keep recalling what the lovely woman in Peebles said to me when she found out my route : "well you're nearly there then!" It was such a wonderful boost, and still keeps me going. As I write I can hear a bird singing "beans, beans, beans". They say things all the time, sometimes a bit more interesting than that.

Evening

It's 5pm. It's become unnaturally warm now, with no wind and strong sun, which is making me worry about an electrical storm a bit since there are dark clouds in the sky. I've set up the bivi in the open for a change under some crags, Craggy Bivi, but there *are* still trees taller surrounding the clearing (should there be lightening). A slight breeze is building and I hope it's going to just push the weather away. If it starts to thunder I'll just abandon camp and head down the hill for a bit.

The view is completely tremendous. I'm above Crainlarich, so about half way up the West Highland Way. This morning was *horrendous* : leg wasting ups and downs on rock promontories alongside the loch for miles and miles. It was a great and unexpected relief after lunch to get onto some tracks, even if they also had steep ascents. One thing here on the WHW is that it isn't muddy like Northumberland. It is mainly rock – which makes its own issues like this morning. Tend to be passing same poeple over and over on the route now, but no problems with it.

Only foraging today was wild garlic (ransom) which happened to be abundant. Other foraging that I have done on Loch Lomond (that doesn't count as natural) is ONE MIDGET GEM on the track and one tissue (unused). I count it as tidying up as much as helping myself. Feeling quite hungry again – this route is taking a toll. Enjoying it when I can get time/distance out of my mind. If I'm enjoying myself the distance passes anyway. Quite careful not to get too breathless on ascents – taking them VERY slowly, otherwise I might not properly recover. I bet this is good 6633 training (an Arctic ultra 'race' where you pull your sled with your gear for hundreds of miles and where it's important not to sweat since it will freeze you).

Mileage today – 15miles. Sticks getting even shorter.

Thursday 27th April. Crainlarich to Loch Tulla. Druim a Bhtair. 'Cuckoo Bivi'

Morning

Think my saliva has stopped working. Constant dry mouth. Look forward to cleaning teeth. Rain came down after 2 or 3ish am. Till then too hot and not sleeping much. Proper downpour tested basha – v.good apart from tendency to stretch. Much better than poncho – with that I would have been at least a bit wet. It has also done very well in high winds – no damage. Feel a bit tired this morning. Dreamed about food: was lulled into a house, went in by mistake and ate. There was some kind of family trip as well where I had coffee and cake. The bit in the house turned into a drama/musical about a person who ate all the pasta so there was none left for the town.

Don't want to get up this morning. Should be heading over Rannoch Moor – quite keen to do that. PROGRESS. Looks like it's mostly on military roads (old ones) from now on – after Tyndrum. That ought to mean using the passes sensibly rather than straight ups and downs over hilltops.

Katy is off school ill at the moment (Andy messaged me). Andy was worried since no message from me. SHOULD HAVE MADE MORE CONTACT. Wanted to make more progress first. Much milder weather now – yesterday VERY WARM but this am still slight cold breeze.

Had small dose of sauerkraut, a few nuts and prunes and some water for breakfast.

Mid-morning

Just had my first cry. Saw a train and turned to look at Ben More and surge of emotion. I've pepped myself up a bit regarding food, thinking actually that I *do* have enough. Thinking about when climbing an 8,000 metre mountain you can't even absorb the food, let alone have enough to eat. You don't get larch needles and sorrel 'sweeties' like that, and water isn't available at all except with huge effort. So really, I'm in good shape for another week. Walking around here (Tyndrum area) there are signs everywhere for drinks, food, shops, places to stay, which is very annoying for me right now.

Lunchtime

I put away my water filter since not had to use it now for days. Makes it simpler to fit water pouch into bumbag. It was a long walk here to Bridge of Orchy this morning. Probably 12miles, but quite enjoyable apart from final 2miles. I'm in the station underpass to shelter since rain started, but concrete is VERY cold.

Evening

Just finished dinner. I love my broth, especially with wild garlic. The only trouble is it takes so long to eat – so much chewing of the dried meat. On way to tonight's bivi saw sign on fence (defaced) saying turn back to campsite since no wild camping on the route. Poo to that! Set up on side of hill by good stream under large scots pine.

Friday 28th April. Loch Tulla to Kinlochleven. 'Grass Bed Bivi'

Morning

Slept really well. Rained on and off all night. Tarp still good. Mists hanging in the valleys this morning. Heard first cuckoo. 'Cuckoo Bivi'. Today is a puzzle – whether to have a short one or push over the hills in the afternoon. Will depend on how I feel and what time I get to Glencoe Ski Resort. If the worst comes of it I *can* sleep overnight on the open hill. Done it many times before. Don't really need to be in Fort William till Sunday since no ferry across Loch Linnhe till Monday.

Used my clothes inside my rucksack liner as a mattress again last night, along with boots and med/bits bag at feet – works well and is becoming the norm. Protection from cold of the ground mainly.

Lunchtime

Long trek this am over Rannoch Moor and Glencoe. All the woods/forests are fenced off. Maybe a good reason (deer fences) but doesn't look/seem right. In all this wildness little bunches of trees/animals corralled, or kept out.

Doing quite well, but aware of big climbs to come. Think I have been quite badly dehydrated using the filter because now peeing more than 2 times/day and mouth not dry all the time/ lips no longer chapped. Obvious really!

Heard reason Katy been off school – pain in stomach is a urichal cyst (apparently to do with umbilical chord severance not healing properly). Seems very symbolic – I go away and something between us showing the effects. I think/learn that she is alright – just bored and on penicillin. Yuk!

Evening

Had a good day in terms of mileage. One of the steep ascents I was dreading – the Devil's Staircase (because of what a few people had said) turned out not to be too bad. My legs seem to prefer steady steep up rather than lots of ups and downs. Starting to be concerned now about walk into Inverie – it's time for that now I suppose.

Today was one stunning view opening up after another and I've been on the camera all day. Couldn't help it. But probably good because it made me keep pausing. Good to go slow. I'm positioned now I think for day to Glen Nevis, but not sure. Just managed to get bivi site set up before customary afternoon rain. The best time for weather is the morning when usually dry and clear apart from hill mist which burns off. Then the afternoons can get a bit warmer, then the evening rain tends to come (and often overnight rain). Rain seems to come a bit earlier here in Ben Nevis' ambit. The weather has become really glorious and ideal most of the time.

Steep climb to 550m today, as well as much else besides. Bivi just outside Kinlochleven.

Saturday 29th April. Kinlochleven to Camusnagaul. 'Primordial Bivi'.

Morning

Another comfortable night. Before dawn the sound of toad/frog on the move. Also that strange, low frequency spring vibrating sounding bird. Grouse also. I've bivied in the open heathland, where I collected lots of dry grass to pad the bed and protect it from the watery moss underneath – Grass Bed Bivi. There are woods all around but they're thinly dispersed, young silver birch and on unsuitably steep slopes. Deciduous trees are now mostly in leaf. It's 5.30am and looks like rain coming. Wind whipped at tarp last night – looked like a kite wanting to take off, but lovely thing held and no damage. Bee/wasp again this morning – as there was last night as well

Afternoon

I'm sitting by the A88 to Inverness in a bus shelter in Fort William, opposite the ferry slipway, having raced to get here to catch the Saturday ferry. Looked so dead when I got here that I phoned the ferry operator to see if any were on. I got here about 1.50pm and the ferry is at 4.15. Don't mind at all.

Thought about it and really didn't want to sit out a whole day in Glen Nevis just because no ferry Sunday. I cut out the last few miles of WHW to take the road so that I could forage something for tonight and get to Fort William on time. Feel tired now and not very hungry. Overdone it. The morning was a bit of a climb out of Kinlochleven, then stunning views over the passes to the Ben. Hard on the feet – gravelly and overlain with large boulders – very slippery and tripping up. Saw first seal in the loch because someone sitting photographing it.

Coastguard search and rescue and fire engine turned up here as I write. Leaving engines running – VERY NOISY. several large motorbikes parked and also engines running – worse. Can't concentrate in all this noise. Moving to sit on the slipway.

As I walk I keep checking now not only for leaves but maybe a dropped sweet!

Let my feet get too sweaty rushing to get here. Hope no blisters. I think I need to eat something – feeling woozy. One thing driving my wish to get to Inverie sooner rather than later is rations – VERY LOW now. Will need to forage a lot.

Evening

Have taken the ferry over to Camusnagaul on the other side of the loch and set up bivi quickly on steep hillside (just before rain again!). It is EXTREMELY lush up here. There's a funny smell, which I suspect is the sheer number of growing things and peat – 'Primordial Bivi' – and it's so wet that I've made a bed of bracken to protect self/gear from seepage from below. I have a view of Ben Nevis (in snow) from here and the bay with yachts, which sounds lovely but also the noises from the town too. Have gulls which I always like (childhood associations with seaside).

MUST FORAGE TOMORROW SINCE OUT OF GREENS AND ROOTS. Should be okay. I have 6 days to do about 40 miles (easy, but some steep ascents and tide allowances at Sourlies). Would like to do the 27km/17m to Glenfinnan tomorrow, but that might not leave enough time to forage.

Just had dinner and all the way through 'The Entertainer' has been playing (just the first few phrases) on what sounds like an ice cream van. Trying to be annoying?

Not sure what I think about my Expedition. Too easy? I only have 3 portions of pemmy left and as good as nothing besides (1 prune and 3 nuts each day – same as the past week in fact). Only the sauerkraut liquid is left – but very precious nutrition. With some foraging it will get me there. I'd like to do it in 3 days or I won't have any pemmy left, although 4 days would be okay since 3 nights only – just so long as I get to Inverie in time for food.

Nighttime

It's quite warm tonight. About 3am now. I've been watching the array of lights in Fort William. The revelries went on late – to 12.30/1ish. I think maybe a party boat? The birds seem to sing all night. Wildlife has really come in abundance over the last few days:

2 red deer yesterday early morning as I left camp – we just stared at each other for ages before they gently stalked away. The seal in the loch. Frogs and toads. Then there's the mouse I have for company that I can hear as I write.

I go to bed so early (as soon as cleared up stove and pots) maybe 6pm if very cold, that being awake early in the morning is just a pleasure. It's nice to lay down with nothing to do. Feeling quite excited now and think less anxious about the days ahead. The whole journey has been full of emotional surges that keep me hopeful – a series of new landmarks that signify the next leg of the route and new territory. For the first time, though, in my expedition(s) I cannot recall the bivis in sequence and retrace it all. There's just too much to take in.

EVENING ROUTINE:

1. Find and tidy site
2. Set up tarp/basha
3. Get gear under tarp
4. Arrange cooking pots
5. Arrange bed roll
6. Change into duvet jacket and hat
7. Take off boots
8. Put on waterproof over trousers and down booties
9. Prep food (chopping etc)
10. Prep ground for stove, preferably on rocks.
11. Light stove and get to heat
12. Fry pemmy
13. KEEP FEEDING STOVE WITH WOOD
14. Put larger pot on with water, leaves, roots and bring to boil
15. Mix in the pemmy
16. Eat
17. Tidy pots and cooled stove
18. Use hot rocks for drying boots and warming sleeping bag

19. Have a pee
20. Take off lower clothes and put into pillow
21. Get legs into sleeping bag.
22. Put duvet jacket in pillow.
23. Lie down
24. Have whisky
25. Write diary
26. SLEEP.

Sunday 30th April. Camusnagaul to Glenfinnan, nr Corryhully Bothy. 'Wallpit Bivi'

Evening

What a bitch of a day. This morning was alright (in fact started quite nice) walking along the Camusnagaul road. I managed to forage a lot of greens, including nettles, which I particularly wanted. Then it occurred to me to collect seaweed. Filled a water bladder with it. Brown weed like kelp. Then the road (an 'A' road with passing places!) became very tedious and cars give no quarter here. They like speed. I suppose to go anywhere they have to go a long way. Got tired of flinging myself into hedges. They seem to like their cars – all v. expensive new 4x4s. Did stop to sit down on side of Loch Eil in the wind – quite relaxing but exposed.

Then the Mallaig road was HORRIBLE. Couldn't see another good way round to Glenfinnan but thought it was a shortish stretch. 5 miles of HELL. Someone stopped and asked me if wanted a lift, which was a nice gesture but disquieting.

When I finally got to Glenfinnan all changed. Tourist area intermingled with backpackers/walkers. Alistair (Ranger here) drove past and stopped for a chat to ask me where I was headed. He was so welcoming. Stressed that camping anywhere not a problem. Made me feel quite well looked after and cosy. Brought me back down to earth after getting worked up about the route. Hot and cold and WINDY and looking like rain (then not) all day again. Have become (made myself become) quite accepting about stop-starts for weather.

Washed my seaweed in Finnan. Also, this am had quite a lucky find. A flower pot (long/deep kind) with a dead tree in it beside the loch. Thistle had taken over. Root all the way to the bottom – all I had to do was tease the compost off the root. Washed in Finnan too.

Set up bivi in forest in a dish made from an old wall (Wallpit Bivi)- but STILL the wind has got up and is rattling through. NEVER GET SHELTER FROM THE WIND.

Monday 1st May. Glenfinnan to Glen Dessary. 'May Day Bivi'

Morning

5.30am. Really excellent night. Low sound of stream tumbling down the hillside by my bivi. Sharp gusts of wind between complete stillness. Cuckoos singing – in fact in the whole of the highlands it's the cuckoos and gulls that I've heard the most of. This is another mossy, tussocky forest, so I was worried about water into my bed, but has stayed nice and dry. Last night for dinner I boiled some seaweed, nettles, thistle root, a few sharper greens and small amount of pemmican fat. VERY FILLING. I'll get there on this ration. Threw away half the bladder of raw seaweed since quite heavy and I'd completely overdone it with quantity. It doesn't seem to boil down to nothing as I'd thought it might.

Thinking of how to take the rest of the journey – slower or faster. Now I have food I can last another 2 days easily, and I'm early for my lift out. Also, 2 more nights means more options for decent bivis and arriving in Inverie at time of day when I can sort myself out. On the other hand, if I have the strength and time to get in to Sourlies tomorrow then I will probably take the option just because it feels wrong to dawdle after all the effort I've already put in. I was quite woozy yesterday (lack of food I think) so I still need to be careful not to lose condition too much – not just rely on the fact I have seaweed now. I think I'll make the decisions as I go.

Lunchtime

9 miles down and 18 to go! Reached Strathan – not a moment too soon. Sunshine is gorgeous but headwind serious all the way from Glenfinnan, and after the tremendous pull over the top of the watershed a bog yomp all the way down. Let's see now. Fell by: slipping once and getting soaked, lost leg in bog up to knee and soaking trouser again, slipped on rock in river when crossing and soaked other trouser leg and sustained cuts/abrasions (bleeding). A bit of a route finding issue and doubled-back from a hairy line round a waterfall. Mainly exhausted from the yomp. The scenery is very primal.

Not surprised, I suppose, to see a few people camping but I immediately thought "how lazy"! When I reflect I don't see why others should all be on a time/distance push like me. Why not just get to the top and camp a few days? Think I might take 3 days over this final stretch to Inverie, just to retain my senses. I don't think I could do another entire afternoon of this after this morning. Having to snack on tiny morsels of pemmy just to have the energy for it.

From Glenfinnan the trail leads you into a false sense of security. It starts on a metalled road on the flat, then rises up and soon going up very steeply (becomes good rubble track). The wind whips over the col into your face and body. When you come over the top it's a great relief at first till you realise it's bog all the way to Strathan. Falls inevitable, route issues inevitable.

IT DOES FEEL QUITE RUGGED NOW – NOT TOO EASY!

Going through the Dessary forest for the route onwards is swampy at first – reminds me of Keilder Forest, Northumberland.

It's 3pm and my camp is set (May Day Bivi). I've decided that 3 days at 9m/day best thing, since that way I can get to Sourlies Bothy at a good time incase I want to use it, and on Weds I can get to Inverie with enough time to eat and sort out where to sleep.

This afternoon turned REALLY hot. Was relieved to find Dessary Forest track since I thought it was going to stay swampy. My boots kept sinking in as well as the poles, and just when I needed a pole for support it would be sinking further and stuck. VILE. I've now got my boots and socks hanging in the sun to dry, though they never do except by sleeping on them. Trousers dry now though, if still muddy. I should have worn my gaiters (which I made specially) but was lulled by the road in and then too absorbed in yomping, and anyway legs already soaked.

My plan is to have early dinner with seaweed and nettle and a bit of pemmy fat.

Later

Now had dinner. Seaweed didn't cook down as much as I'd wanted. Found out late in the day that adding a splash of sauerkraut juice adds some flavour (salt). Put hot rocks from under stove in boots to try and dry them. Have a trickling stream next to my bivi in Dessary Forest (May Day Bivi) – very soothing and handy.

Tuesday 2nd May. Glen Dessary to Sourlies Bothy, Loch Nevis

Morning

Having a later morning. Woke at 4.30ish and dozed till 5.00. Getting up now at 6.00 (almost 12 hours in bed!). Have been sleeping really well, which I think has a lot to do with how well I'm feeling (apart from hunger, now allayed a lot with seaweed). Had quite a lumpy night with uneven, stony ground which I did my best to relieve with bits of kit, but still a bit awkward. I FIND THAT ALL THE TIME, EVEN LYING AWAKE, I HAVE THE LITTLE RHYTHM THAT GOES THROUGH MY HEAD WHEN I WALK STILL GOING ON.

I don't have the excitement for getting to Inverie that I've felt earlier in the expedition. Not sure why, since it's getting so close. I know I have 2 passes to cross with a lot of tough ascent – but it's pain that will pass (fairly) quickly. Tonight might be my last bivi night.

I'm thinking how to eke out food. Plenty of seaweed and greens but no pemmy to speak of – one small piece – essentially for 2 days' work. I need to use 2/3rds of it today and save 1/3 for my walk into Inverie. Better portion it up. If sauerkraut juice runs out I'll need for the first time to mix a dioralyte from the med kit to keep safe tomorrow given the heat.

Afternoon

Morning was an awful boggy pull (slow and sustained) away from Dessary forest (seemed to go on forever). I had a spell of hopelessness – worry about lack of food and no energy at all to carry on. Had a sit down and small nibble of pemmy fat eventually, and that together with opening views seemed to change my spirits. Decided to take regular breaks and remind myself that I had all day for 9 miles if I wanted it. A deer was lain down as I approached large boulders and only saw me late on. I followed it around boulder, where it stood with another above me. Taking time out to watch them and take pictures lifted my spirits. Took some more deep plunges into bogs – downheartening. When terrain flattened I felt instantly stronger and began really enjoying the day. The Rock is monumental, and so crystalline and full of shiny minerals that it grips the feet well and sparkles in the light. Magical. Sun got VERY strong – really hot – to the point that I tucked away my primaloft! Could feel my nose burning, blisters forming, but no sunblock (in bin at Galashiels!).

After the watershed things got very much better – more rock than peat and moss underfoot. Beautiful tarn/loch on the prow with nice picky scramble through the funnel where it emerged as a waterfall down towards Loch Nevis. MUCH easier descent than the one to Strachan. Much craggier. The only nasty bit was on the flat towards the Sourlies Bothy. Marsh.

IDYLL – Bothy in the sunshine by the sea.

There's a lot of leafy foraging around the Bothy, and I collected a variety of different seaweeds for dinner as well. Made seaweed soup up for tomorrow at same time. Now feel much happier that stomach is provided for and I'll have the energy to make it. Have to leave early so the tide will be full out (6am should be okay according to man I met sunbathing outside his tent in vicinity) – so I can walk around the bay and up to the river crossing.

When I entered the Bothy 2 bunks taken with kit lain out – occupants arrived later having been walking locally. Seems like a popular place to use as a base – NOT SURPRISING. Good guys, good chats.

Outside the Bothy there are heaps of large muscle shells and a big fire pit. Couldn't forage any – shame. Still, my soup had much more flavour today and I feel restored.

The guys are packing now waiting for tide-out since they plan to walk to Inverie tonight. Don't think I would, but I'm bushed anyhow. Another couple arrived, saw occupants of Bothy and left to set up camp quite a distance away! So looks as though maybe only me here tonight. That would be good so I can sleep early and leave early without disturbing anyone.

Nighttime

Was just settling down and noises began outside. Thought it must be someone coming down to Bothy but no sign of anyone. Then started again so thought birds on the roof or rats – that maybe someone had left rubbish outside and attracted them. But the noise got quite loud. Went outside and saw herd of deer – maybe them?? Gets more idyllic every moment!

Finding being in Bothy quite nice. Not nearly so exhausting as when I have to do the evening routine after scouting out a bivi. It's easy living! This Bothy is also clean and dry – I suppose easier in the sea air on the beachside than on the eternally wet helm wind of Cross Fell, Cumbria. I'm hoping the climb out of here tomorrow will be on the nice dry rock rather than peat and moss bogs.

Finding it hard to know how I feel at this stage. Was expecting to feel quite emotional at the end but I don't think I will. I think that moment came earlier – at points when I realised how far I'd come and what was left to do – especially when I thought that I might just succeed. I tried so hard to make sure that I wouldn't be defeated by the mileage in this last week that I've made things (relatively) easy for myself. That said, today I wanted to give up on the climb up from the forest. I think I might be too exhausted perhaps to connect with the Expedition as a whole. I don't know. I'm feeling quite daunted by trying to take it in and reflect upon it. Usually I'm itching to do that right away.

Now that I'm feeling properly fed the urgency for completing has faded. I was looking forward to getting to Inverie and mooching about, having some different food, but now not so enthusiastic about it. The two men in here earlier were quite negative about spending time there with nothing to do. I hope I don't feel like that. I had been up to now driven by the notion of having nowhere to go and nothing to do – A HOLIDAY! I hope there is somewhere I can get a present for Katy that means something – I want that to be in Inverie. I'm not sure I want to be in a B&B as they are going to be.

Maybe a camp site will be okay if I can leave some of my stuff and go and look around.

If the weather stays good, some time on the beach!? I do feel the cold quite badly though now when I'm not exerting myself.

Wednesday 3rd May. Sourlies Bothy to Inverie. 'Glitter Beach Bivi'.

Morning

It's 4am and I'm awake in the Bothy – as I have been all night on account of the loudest mouse in the western world. It sounds like someone is preparing a meal on the table opposite. So decided to get up and write. Was thinking about yesterday and what to call the scramble thing that I enjoyed so much. Must have been a gorge really – where the tarns/little lochs released water through steep-sided gully down into a waterfall. Had to keep crossing the water from side to side when the rock walls got too steep. Canyoning then!? I'm in love with this rock. Found myself being quite skilled with my old climbing moves, even now with my pack on (most of the time!). Just like walking in to the Obergablehorn with friend Ian, quite a few years ago though, had to throw pack off for some moves then haul it. I went EXTREMELY carefully (aka slowly). An accident out here is no simple matter to remedy... and alone...

In fact on my way towards Strathan from Glenfinnan I heard about one of a pair resting in a tent who was injured and was going to have to try and get himself back over the pass I'd just come down. Bloody nightmare. Sobering. I don't think I could do this terrain carrying an injury – on top of arthritis that is.

Looking forward to today, except a bit concerned about getting the tide right.

Thinking that in Inverie I might make for campsite rather than B&B – even if it IS full of kids playing football as man sunbathing had found. Oh for a pod or cabin! – esp. since I could then leave stuff to meander about. Probably going to be tired after no sleep tonight. Good job I stayed away from bothies etc till now.

Had my first poo in weeks this am. Looked like deer scat.

Just packed ready to go and watching tide. Feels strange to me not to have been meticulous about packing. Noticed that I left a striker[30] outside last night while cooking my soup – getting TOO RELAXED!

Afternoon

THE BIG DAY. I left about 6am and was just right to get across the bay to the (dangerous) bridge. Unfortunately then it all went horribly wrong. A combination of things. I'd been looking at some maps left in the Bothy at a much larger scale than my own. More detail was also more misleading. But biggest problem was the map directed me right of the ruined farm buildings at Carnoch rather than left. So I ended up on a wild goose chase picking up paths that led into swamp (quite serious swamp – dangerous to be around). I started looking for boot marks and saw only animal tracks. I KNEW that the route went straight up – I'd been looking at the close contours for days and wondering if I had the strength. Wonder how I could have considered heading out on the flat!! Trouble was, along with the maps, the two fellas last night in the Bothy left at 6pm saying they'd be in the pub in Inverie before closing. I thought it was about 9 miles, so they probably couldn't but now had in my head that it couldn't be that difficult. Those factors, along with the tiredness brought on by Bothy mouse, and long term hunger, as well as the habit of following boot prints along the trails, had me heading up the swampy valley.

After about an hour I decided to quit and head back to Carnock, after first trying to make up a new route to Inverie from where I

---

30   Fire steel used to make sparks for lighting tinder.

thought I must now be according to map/compass work. I had to do some careful picking around the bogs, then back at Carnock a simple left line took me straight up the side of the hill.

I was pleased with myself that despite stupid navigation to begin with I just took it on the chin and started again. It was still only 9ish in the morning.

When I started on the right route I heard the voices of the two guys from last night behind me. The main man not nearly so friendly. During the day as we crisis-crossed each other the greetings got warmer. The climb was about 600m and I really enjoyed it. It helped that I could feed myself every so often with seaweed broth.

The walk down the other side got even more blisteringly hot so it was hard work, but with a thrilling view of the sea and woods of Inverie. Nose burned really badly. Stopped at a stream 1 mile out of Inverie to wash armpits and change upper clothes, so that I could just go into a tea shop straight away.

Inverie is UNIQUE and absolutely beautiful. Not much in the way of services (and no phone network), but what's here is good. Good ethics.

I had haggis and baked potato, which I found surprisingly easy to eat – VERY GOOD SIGN OF HEALTH. I never lost my appetite at all except at the end of the West Highland Way when I pushed hard to get to the ferry. Campsite easygoing – log cabin with turf roof, compost toilet in another cabin with turf roof. Lots of things invited to help self to and pay on honesty basis. Odd place (and charming). Workshops tucked away. I've pitched at the end of the campsite near bird hide overlooking estuary, in a little copse. Glimpsed a small boat or two in a bay behind me. Can hear gentle sound of woodworking (tapping). The sand on the beach in front of me is soft, grey and sparkles. Will go to the pub (a long walk) to try and get wifi.

Later

Pub not open Wednesday but Rangers' hut open all the time with free wifi. Knoydart is like God's reward for doing the walk. My boots are still sparkling with Knoydart rock dust.

6

After The Walking Stopped

Diary Entries

Thursday 4th May 2017

Evening

Been a social day – talking to a lot of people about my expedition, letting information in by degrees. Sat outside the pub this evening in the sunshine, along with many more folk. A Glaswegian guy there came to talk to me. He noticed I mentioned bushcraft and said 'We've all been down that route and left it behind – It's all fat blokes sitting round fires.' Didn't mention Farafoot, where there are women too and no fat blokes. Wonder where he did his bushcraft. He said he'd seen my bivi up at the end of the campsite and told me there are otters up there, on the estuary. He also asked me if I knew there was someone living there, just a few feet away from me. I didn't. He is doing up his boat in the little bay behind me (I had noticed that!). Anyhow, he said he'd come to talk to me because 'its nice to meet someone doing some shit.' I like that. He said he likes Rum and Skye, and comes over here a lot.

More conversations at the pub, and I find myself being quite open since everyone else is.

I have had two pints of 'Remoteness' ale, the only food I could get (packet of chilli peanuts), and I've foraged greens on the mile-or-so walk back to my bivi. It seems the Forge pub restaurant is out of action due to bereavement in chef's family.

I was talking to a couple doing some of the Cape Wrath trail. They said they were here 20 years ago (or maybe it was 10 years that they said) on New Year's Eve. They came over on the ferry, were booked at the pub for food, but found pub not serving and ended up in the kitchen of a local being served venison stew. They are from the Brecons, and he is a fell/ultra distance runner. I got into an absorbing conversation with his partner about bunions and the agonies they inflict. Recommended my boots.

Met a climber/walker from Falkirk, there with a friend to do some routes. He turned out to be a fell runner too, his physio being the inspirational fell champion Angela Mudge. He and his friend and others have recently started the 45 degree mountaineering club.

WHAT AN INSPIRING BUNCH OF PEOPLE TO HAPPEN ACROSS.

Friday 5th May

Morning

Went to the snack van this morning for breakfast. Had portobello mushroom and garlic halloumi in a large bap. Free tea refil. Wonderful. Rather more than your standard snack van. Was approached there by another couple who'd heard about my foraging. Also got back into conversation with the couple from Brecon. We got straight into bunion stories again! She's been having treatment for years and years. She was persuaded against surgery because they were going to put plates in her toes that would prevent flexing. Instead she wears footbeds. I feel very relieved that the boots work for me. Had yet another foot conversation with a young Bavarian woman hiking here alone. She is having a day off because her rigid mountain boots aren't suitable for the terrain and are wrecking her feet. I noticed she had rock climbing boots on to rest her feet – ouch! Not exactly slippers.

Love being able to leave my things just lying around here. Feels completely safe in every way. Locals set the tone with use of honesty boxes.

Still hearing cuckoos all the time. Will forever after be nostalgic when I hear them, just as I am for the Pennines when I hear grouse.

Had a newborn baby kind of poo this morning – green, but thankfully not smelly! (Sorry – these kind of details take on some significance when I'm 'out there'.)

Evening

I'm sunbathing on the beach – on the west coast of Scotland, in early May! I am so well recovered that I feel like going for a run. I think that's just my glee expressing itself. Lying here looking up at the hills they look comforting – soft, like antler velvet. This place feels like my Burgh Island of the North[31](notwithstanding their utter difference, both humane places of sanctuary).

---

31 Burgh Island is a small island on the Devon coast, near Kingsbridge, east of Plymouth (my birthplace, incidentally). The island is connected to the mainland by a causeway that cuts it off when the tide comes in. Perched on it is a 1920s hotel that celebrates the Art Deco of its time and the civilised living. We love to stay there for the food and the sea and the sheer fun.

Friday late

Met another man (from Manchester) staying on the campsite who is doing the Corbetts (now he has done all the Munros)[32]. Told me he was at the Sourlies Bothy 10 years ago and there was a mouse who notoriously stole food. The mouse at Sourlies is, apparently, legendary (and its descendants too obviously). NOBODY sleeps in the bothy because of the noise – they all end up outside (except myself then and probably a few other folk who have their own reasons for staying under the roof).

Friendly couple I met in the tea room yesterday also arrived in the pub. She has a sun allergy so is finding the weather difficult!

Saturday 6th May

Morning

Over the past few days have spent quite a bit on presents and a 'Trophy' pottery chalice for myself. Want to mark this occasion. Have also spent quite a bit on drink since ale is almost £5 per pint at the pub.

As I'm writing, lying in my bivi bag, there is a squeaking and the flattened grasses in front of me move in a ripple across my eyeline. The sun is just coming up behind me.

The Forge last night were miraculously serving food but were fully booked so the proprietor said. He is a very tall Belgian showing no hospitality. The band who were booked to play (and to eat I think) went outside when they got no food, nor audience. He complained about the way our group (myself, the 45 degree club, and the Corbetts climber) were occupying tables, although the pub

---

32 Munros, Corbetts and Marilyns are names for mountains distinguished by their heights and relative heights to their surroundings, Munros being the highest, of which Ben Nevis is one.

was nearly empty, and removed my stick saying it was dangerous (I do see his point there since it kept falling over, still his manner didn't help). Eventually he offered food to the man from Manchester who'd had the ambition to try and get fed there – soup and mussels since he obviously had some left over, but was annoyed when he at first couldn't decide if he wanted both soup and mussels. (I've since discovered that soup and mussels are all anyone can ever get there, if they are lucky enough to get served anything at all!)

I took the Western Isles ferry at 10.45am. Was ready to go hours early, thinking it would be hard to lug my pack the mile or so up the road, but when I lifted it it felt light, and I strong (with even a heavy croc bottle of gin now in there). Said my so-longs to the 45 degree mountaineering club and went and waited at the wonderful tea room/pottery (which I found didn't open till 10 on Saturday). Was longing for a word from home but nothing, so disappointed.

People kept turning up with bags and they were all fretting over whether they'd have time for breakfast before the ferry. I got influenced and started to worry too whether I might miss out on my cup of tea. Tried to stop myself being silly and thinking 'I was here first!' They annoyed me with talking about vacuum cleaners, but I didn't want to shift and lose my place as first in the queue. I thought, had Andy been with me he would have let everyone in before us – another good reason to do these things alone!!

Another couple came and sat opposite me. Assumed they'd annoy me too but liked them. We got talking. They asked me about my walk but didn't say much about themselves. Learned they were from Perth, but only when he got talking with the couple from Brecon I learned that he is a very experienced climber/mountaineer.

There seems to be a type of Scots male climber – stout and hardy looking with an intensity about them that isn't expressed verbally except when they look at a hill and start talking about it. They don't have airs and affectations, just knowledge gained on the ground.

On the boat he and the Brecon climber/runner viewed and

discussed the Cuillin (ridge on Skye) and gave me goose pimples saying the gabbro (type of rock) is good but you have to be really careful because of the sheer drops and the loose bits. It's been a while since I've climbed with that level of exposure, but you don't expect chossy rock on Skye (that's a feature more in the Alps). He said he had to concentrate really hard there. Such an easy-going and relaxed person who seemed to know the entire west coast area in great detail. I've been really impressed in Inverie with the dedication of the walkers and climbers to the region, but their quiet confidence rather than bravado. Bravado would go down very badly in Knoydart.

I took a ridiculous number of pictures of the Isles: Rum and Eigg but mostly Skye. You could see the black and red Cuillin, but it's hard to do them justice in a photo from a boat.

Sunday 7th May

Morning

Arriving in Mallaig on the ferry yesterday I could feel myself getting emotional, turning my back to everyone incase I cried. Sister, Louise, and Mum were at the ferry terminal, so by the time I'd found them it had worn off. IT WAS LOVELY TO SEE THEM and to see that they looked so chilled. Lou took the Morar coastal route out and we ogled the views. It was what Mum called a 'Brigadoon day' (from the film where a place appears only sporadically and so can't be returned to at will), referring to the rarity of this kind of weather in the Highlands and Islands. Sunbathing and PADDLING/SWIMMING! going on in the gorgeous bays.

We made for Glenfinnan (very odd to arrive by car) to have a drink. Then Lou set-to taking pictures of me on her made-for-the-job iPhone 7 for the film credits! (She said you always need a good picture of the actual person for the film credits and we need to take it before the 'look' wears off!)

When I saw myself in the mirror – just my face – I was quite shocked and worried that perhaps I wasn't as healthy as I thought. I even had an emotional moment thinking 'sorry Andy, sorry Katy, I've gone too far', anticipating their shock. Lou reassured me, though, that actually I look strong and healthy, and just like someone who's done something monumental. She talked about her wild swim (when she went to Mexico) and how it was possibly the best experience of her life. I feel that way about this. LIFE CHANGING MOMENTS.

Lou took us to the Argyll Hotel in central Glasgow for Saturday night. It feels completely acceptable to come to the centre of a bustling city after the solitude – in a way that going to a duller, smaller town wouldn't. In fact it's a bit like going to Kathmandu after Everest – there's the charm of the contrast (and the relief of safety). And even more similarly, all night I've had the window open (so nice to have a hotel window that can be properly opened) and the life on the street hasn't stopped. The funny thing is that there are some characters who've stayed put and been talking to various others, who've come and then left, all night. They've been talking in such broad Glaswegian accents, though, that I haven't known what it's all about – it's like listening to music (with high points in expletives and emotional renditions), or listening to birds. I loved it. I did sleep, but not very much. I don't mind at all.

We went walking off last night to find somewhere to eat but everywhere local and suitable for us was fully booked. We ended up in Sauchihall Street (infamous according to mum), in an Indian street food restaurant (called Tuk Tuk). Loved it. They didn't serve alcohol but would just charge corkage for your own. I was happy to go without. Will have that kind of celebration (a toast) with Andy. Felt quite right to be having street food to celebrate completion, especially with the spiritual aspects so strong. I've borrowed some pantaloon style leggings from Lou, after being unimpressed with the bag put together for me (not sure whether by me or Andy – I forget). With my hazel pole and big boots I look like a yesteryear gentlewoman climber. All I need is a hemp rope over my shoulder.

Over the course of the day yesterday in catch-up discussions I learned that actually Katy had been in hospital in the later stages of my expedition because the penicillin for her urichal cyst hadn't worked and she needed IV antibiotics. There had been a debate over whether I should be informed and brought home. Lou's view was that, since Katy didn't have a high or low temp there wasn't a need, and that the consequences could be bad for all of us to let me know unnecessarily – guilt, regret, blame etc. Andy agreed but had the task of mediating everyone's views. So glad they understood, and of course that Katy is so thoughtful and resiliant. (Andy since told me that I was out of range anyway by then so they couldn't have let me know.)

When I looked in the full size mirror in my room it shocked me to see my body, more that it had to see my face. I look starved. I'm not sure that I've ever been so thin (not even after Everest). It's a bit scary. I even thought I need to put on some fat immediately.

I find, though, in this semi-starved state I feel quite attuned to things – I can feel my emotions and my thoughts acutely. It's a phenomenon that is brought up frequently when you're fully immersed in nature, especially when enduring physical hardship. Maybe only the natural world is big enough to overpower the ego. As Byrd felt, I agree that 'these are the best times, the times when neglected senses expand to an exquisite sensitivity' from 'Alone: The Classic Polar Adventure' by Richard E. Byrd. So perhaps there is a big difference between the anorexic starvation and the fasting ascetic – in the impacts and state of mind. I know that when I was younger and in an anorexic state I used to get euphoric (so maybe no difference), but it was driven by unhappiness and insecurity. This leanness has brute strength underpinning it, and a direction for the future. It is something to grow and learn from.

I'm sitting in my (noisy) hotel bedroom window writing and

watching people. They all bounce. The morning runners bounce/prance delicately, and pedestrians take jaunty steps to wherever. Is this the effect of the sunshine? Do they grit their teeth, heads down and set against the elements, in the winter? Or is it the Glaswegian swagger? – habitual and maybe even obligatory. It's Sunday morning and still no sleep goes on. Since dawn and before they've all been on the move. The road sweeper truck has just done a bit of a pavement clean-up (8am), making some sort of demarcation between last night and this morning.

Looks like another gorgeous day as we prepare to travel back home – weather which apparently we are taking back down to Shropshire with us after miserable conditions all week!

One week after returning home

Travelling home was an exciting time to wonder over the distances between points in the walk. The occasional Irishly-inflected comment went through my head – so that phenomenon hasn't worn off yet!

Then there was a gorgeous welcome from Andy and Katy, with a card and a cake from Katy. The alcoholic toast finally happened, and in style too! Half a case of champagne from Bob (Andy's dad, but I prefer to say my father-in-law), and much congratulations. But I had nothing at all from my loving Labrador, Faffy. I mean NOTHING. Not even the kind of glance that she'd give an uninteresting stranger. She ducked under my hand when I tried to stroke her. I take it from this that she DID recognise me, but preferred not to acknowledge me. She only forgave me when I took her out for a run.

The run! It wasn't one really. We are both at square one again. I have nothing in my legs for running, and she has too much round her belly. I suppose that my fitness now is very different: low intensity, endurance. We will get faster again together.

The fitness effort is continuing, and I've been intrigued to know what kind of physiological impacts there have been. My body fat mass is 7.9kg, which is quite low – not ideal for staying healthy. The weight loss is obvious (down by a stone), as well as the muscle definition, but I'm a bit horrified by the loss of over an inch (3cm) in height. I NEED TRACTION! It's probably a mixture of dehydration and compression of the discs from the weight of the pack – hopefully impermanent.

I've had an MRI scan of my spine since coming home that was booked before I left due to some sensation loss in my left leg (I have check-ups every two years to follow up from my broken back in 2003). It will be interesting to see if there is anything noteworthy happening.

Two weeks after returning home

My habit of grinding my teeth when I'm asleep seems to have returned, after none during the expedition. I don't like how my head feels after a night of muscle tension in my jaw, which encourages me to start planning the next expedition (extreme self-medication?!).

Notwithstanding the teeth grinding annoyance I'm still feeling the calming effects of the walk, even to the extent that I feel quite happy with our ramshackle little house and it's outdated (and many broken) facilities. I'm reminded why we bought it – because it feels like our very own mountain hut: our bothy.

Postscript: Living Off-Grid in Gometra

Gometra is one of a diminishing number of privately owned islands in Scotland. It sits across the Sound of Mull, connected by a causeway to the Island of Ulva. Within the same month of my arrival back from Knoydart Andy ventured there, on foot for the twenty miles or so from the Mull ferry to the Ulva ferry, and the further eight rugged miles to the bothy on Gometra. He was in time to have some of the glorious weather that I'd enjoyed in Inverie, and similarly chose to sleep under the stars.

Moving to Gometra was an idea that came about after I found the island website and saw that Roc, the owner, had searched for people to live there in the past. As well as the magnificence of the terrain, and views of Staffa and Iona, it offers space, the opportunity (necessity in fact) to innovate, and the chance to live a less mediated life. There is no power supply there, only limited telecoms, and no services. Those facts are scary yet invigorating, and my feelings about it echo this. One of the reasons to move is my sense of being vegetative in Ditton Priors, and no doubt in any other village or town, because of ease of living. I appreciate convenience as much as the next person, but since returning from my expedition I've been starting to feel that everything is futile. Consumerism has a way of sapping the humanity from life. It also involves you in endless meaningless complications. I don't want to expend myself on procuring goods and services from faceless corporations, playing the system. I'm a simple kind of person, who would like straightforward, equitable, transactions and relationships.

Gometra is a testing ground for these ideals, and for our fortitude as a family. The first time I saw Roc was on a recording where he was speaking out against proposed giant salmon farms that would disturb the ecology around Gometra. Andy went on to discover more about Roc's ethics when he visited in May 2017, and particularly Roc's aim to reduce fossil fuel consumption. He walks the eight miles each way to the ferry, although he is accepting of the limited use of quad bikes and cars, since it would be hard to live there without. The few cottages and bothies on the island used to have power via a generator, but now are entirely without electricity. Heating and cooking are achieved using wood burning stoves.

Water comes from the hills overlooking the cottages. As well as evidence of past electrical supplies (sockets on the walls and light switches), there is also evidence of defunct telecoms (telegraph poles with missing wires). There are, though, black plastic pods sticking up from the ground at occasional intervals and these, we've since learned, are lines that can still be connected. There is no reliable mobile network, but signals can be 'chased' to a few spots of connectivity (a distance away from the buildings).

Added to these scarcities, there is no medical service to the island, and no school. So home schooling looks to be the most practical option, but to be potentially isolating for Katy.

We knew most of these things before we set out to see Gometra for ourselves, and the walks across Ulva for the ferry confirmed in our minds that this was a tough proposition.

On our walk in we stopped at Ballacoich to get out from the rain and have a look in the Gometra gallery. Rhoda makes art and jewellery which she sells there, and my thoughts, as much as I could have any in the sodden and painful state that I was in, was that it would be a good place for me to sell walking sticks (hazel with antler handles), and maybe my own wood gas burning stoves.

Arriving at the bothy (Teacher's Bothy) was a great relief, but more so once Andy had lit the stove. With fire anything is possible!

Turning out the food from our packs was a bit embarrassing to us, since our excess was staring us in the face. There was a very heavy Christmas pudding, (made for us by Marjorie Jones in the village a few years previously), cheeses, salamis, tinned mackerel, breads, couscous, rocket salad, naked bars, pearl barley, porridge, fruit and nut mix, dried milk, wine, whisky, cordial, tea and coffee. I think that was all! As well as all that weighing us down we had a rope, harnesses, helmets and gear to try out the rock (though the weather put paid to that idea for a while). Then there were the clothes and sleeping bags. We were, all three, pack ponies serving our prodigious appetites!

After eating and drying through we played a memory game, and settled to a night of good sleep. Katy had the heated lounge then swapped into the bedroom in the morning when we got up.

I slowly got used to ignoring the switches and looking to torches and the stove for light and heat. The one thing we should have brought was candles, and these will now figure highly on my wish-lists. I must make some.

The bothy is south facing, with a window in each room letting in the light from the south. The walls are clad with timber slats, and the floors are painted concrete with rugs. Works well for this terrain of heather, boggy pastures and sandy beaches.

There were no cleaning materials in the bothy, just a few millimetres of washing up liquid and a small bar of soap, so I was concerned about not being able to leave it as pristine as we found it. We covered the couch with our emergency storm shelter to protect the fabric. When you have walked in that far you get an appreciation of the labour involved in bringing anything to these few cottages, so the need to conserve what there is and remove any waste is paramount.

We met Roc quite soon. He came to the door and after talking outside for a while it occurred to me to invite him in for coffee. He didn't drink coffee though, and unknown to us at the time we couldn't have produced it anyhow. We had to reverse engineer the espresso pot since there wasn't enough heat on the stove to push the water up the spout and onto the coffee grounds. So we proceeded tentatively with the conversation, trying not to be presumptuous but wanting to be very clear how keen we were to come to some arrangement for living on his island. Later on his daughters came to the bothy to see whether Katy wanted to go to the beach then go to the 'big house' to play a game. She was unsure at first, but was keen to take one of the live winkles that she'd accidentally collected with her shells back to its home on the beach. They were very understanding, saying that they had had a viking burial ceremony for a prawn once upon a time. In fact they had lots of lovely illustrative anecdotes from their childhood on Gometra that appealed to Katy and ourselves alike.

Katy's care over the life of the winkle meant that the ones I'd collected to eat were instead restored to the beach. Quite right too given the excess of food that we had.

In the end we spent both an afternoon and an evening at Gometra house, playing a board game that afternoon, leaving under cover of umbrellas lent to us, then going for supper the next. In the intervening time we managed to do some rock climbing on the valley of the 'Lost Harbour' (a name given by Roc's children I think) since the weather had improved. Every excursion we made, though, incorporated scavenging trips to the beach for driftwood to burn in the stove. Andy took a bowsaw blade and rigged it to some hazel sticks with paracord, and this allowed him to cut up sizeable timbers. There were many of these which, Rhoda told us, came in a spate recently. Roc confirmed our sense of the abundance of the beach, saying that when he needs something he just has to look on the beach and he'll find it – which is quite magical since the beaches are in no way littered.

My hands became very wet through my leather gloves, which stained them dark blue. This led us to see ourselves as Edward Lear's Jumblies, with heads green and hands blue, living in lands 'Far and Few' and going to sea in a sieve. We thought of naming our new climbing crag 'Chankly Bore' after their adventures there. My own climb I have called 'Rock Lobster' after the clawing straddle of a protruding rib of rock.

I have so far avoided Scotland in the summer through fear of the midges, since I have a very strong histamine reaction. And this proved to be the case. The bites don't bother me too much for about 12 hrs, but then they increase in intensity and get me scratching and irritable. I'll have to sort that out.

Katy's confidence grew as we climbed, despite the fact that some chunks of rock would come off in our hands. We had to test every hold and take a lot of care over protecting ourselves.

The next day we ventured out to have a chat with Rhoda. She was in her magnificent polytunnel, and invited us to sit there with her in the warmth, surrounded by vines, figs and pots of picked raspberries.

Our dogs would have had the lot, but hers were more restrained (well behaved). Rhoda is the only resident here continuously. Her daughter, young Rhoda, is the shepherdess, but lives off Gometra. We were interested to hear from her what it might be like to school Katy, and about the implications of the sale of Ulva. She told us that the community are bidding to buy, but it is a long and involved process. At the agreed time for supper we went to Gometra house but found nobody there. We sat outside, a contribution of fruits and nuts in hand, then eventually went away again. We returned half an hour later to waving arms from Roc, welcoming us in. A meal by candlelight of lentils, cabbage and vegetable tart, followed by apple crumble along with several glasses of cider, had us feeling very happy. We continued the delicate conversation, aware that our future here depended upon it, but helped by the composure and style of our hosts.

By our final day on Gometra we had a proposal for a three year tenancy in the Shepherd's Cottage, renovating it as part of our contribution. Before that, though, spending some trial periods living there to see whether it works for us. We left our spare food in the Shepherd's Cottage Rayburn (to protect from mice), as well as the bowsaw blade, and asked Rhoda to take care of our Christmas pudding till we need it in December. The next thing to arrange is a vessel to cross the waters between Mull and Ulva in the off-season.

Appendices

Appendix One: Food Rations

Leg Two Food Ration:

Sauerkraut 650g, oatcakes 291g, 30 tea bags, pemmican 260g, nut/fruit 260g, whisky, coffee powder

Leg Three Food Ration:

Pemmican: 1kg lean beef, cut thinly and dried then crumbed and bound in 400g of fat
Sauerkraut: 1kg
Dried fruit: 500g
1 lemon
Drinks: coffee, tea, mint tea, hot chocolate.

Leg Four Food Ration:

Homemade sauerkraut: 3 litres (3Kg)
Homemade pemmican: 2kg lean beef, cut thinly and dried then crumbed and bound in 3.5kg of fat
Hazelnuts: 300g
Prunes: 700g
Whisky

Appendix Two: Kit List and Packing

Expedition Leg One: Trial/Initiation Leg

32 litre pack – 11kg when packed
Plastic bag rucksack liner
Ski Pole
Bumbag

Clothes Worn:

Lightweight full zip trousers, wicking teeshirt, lightweight
fleece (full zip), summer weight buff, smart wool socks,
trekking sandals, breathable & waterproof hat with peak
and neck panel (in bumbag when not needed), sunglasses,
watch.

Bumbag:

Compass, maps, tinted reading glasses, sunblock, vaseline,
phone, purse (cash and card), Leatherman knife, head
torch, whistle.

Rucksac:

Main Cavity

Lightweight waterproof jacket, primaloft (lightweight
insulated jacket), waterproof trousers, gloves, thermarest,
underwear, 2 spare pairs walking socks, mammut long
sleeve top, silk tee (for sleeping), silky long johns (for
sleeping), travel towel. Three season sleeping bag, bivi bag,
plastic survival bag cut to make ground sheet.
Mosquito/midge face mask used as a bag for bits: wipes,

tissues, talc, toothbrush and paste, deodorant, alum block (good antiseptic and deodorant), insect repellent, antibacterial dry wash, cotton buds, nail file, nail clippers, lube, 3 extra head torch batteries, duct tape, string, sewing kit, reflective squares, comb and mirror).

Medical/emergency kit: ibuprofen, paracetamol, diazepam (in the event of back spasms), tick removal tool, micropore tape, hydrocortisone, crepe bandage, dioralyte, elastoplast, wound dressing, tweezers, safety pins, handwarmers, insect repellant wipes, lymecycline for rosacea, finacea skin cream for rosacea.

Lid:

Water purifying bottle, whisky, pemmican, oatcakes.

Zip Pocket under lid:

Writing book, maps, pencils, sharpener, pen, eraser.

Expedition Leg Two: 'Sickness Leg'

70 litre pack with plastic liners inside the two cavities
Ski pole with micro towel attached
Plastic trowel (attached with a clip to the pack and tucked into sleeve pocket on pack)

Clothes Worn:

Lightweight Craghopper trousers, wicking teeshirt, lightweight fleece (full zip), primaloft jacket, summer weight buff, smart wool socks, ankle gaiters, half shank goretex-lined leather mountain boots, fleece gloves (in bumbag when not needed), breathable & waterproof hat with peak and neck panel (in bumbag when not needed), sunglasses, watch.

Bumbag:

Compass, maps, water filter bottle (Sawyer system – faster delivery than bottle used in trial), tinted reading glasses, sunblock, vaseline, phone, purse (cash and card), lightweight penknife.

Rucksac

Main Cavity:

Poncho, winter weight Craghopper trousers, triple layer goretex jacket, mountaineering mittens, waterproof trousers, thermarest, bag of clothes (underwear, 3 spare pairs walking socks, spare cap hat, silk glove liners, Lycra shorts, winter buff, spare gloves, long sleeve top, mammut long sleeve top, mammut short sleeve top, silk tee for sleeping, silky long johns for sleeping, travel towel, cacoon liner for sleeping bag (adds a season in terms of warmth), mosquito/midge face mask used as a bag for bits (matches, charge monkey for phone, phone charging cable, tampons, dry shampoo, talc, all purpose biodegradable soap, deodorant, alum block (good antiseptic and deodorant), insect repellent, antibacterial dry wash, cotton buds, nail file, nail clippers, lube, 6 extra head torch batteries, duct tape, string, sewing kit).

Medical/emergency kit: ibuprofen, paracetamol, diazepam (in the event of back spasms), allergy pills, tick removal tool, micropore tape, hypodermic needles, reflective squares, hydrocortisone, moleskin dressing, crepe bandage, dioralyte, elastoplast, wound dressing, second skin dressing, wound closure strips, tweezers, safety pins, handwarmers, insect repellent wipes, hormone tablets and patches, lymecycline for rosacea, finacea skin cream for rosacea.

Bottom Cavity:

Three season sleeping bag, tent pegs, bivi bag, plastic survival bag cut to make ground sheet.

Lid:

Food, spare water bottle for filter.

Zip Pocket under lid:

Writing book, maps.

Side Pocket 1:

Filter-cleaning syringe, pocket gas stove, gas, lighter, leather gloves, tin mug, lid, folding plastic cup, spoon (personal favourite horn spoon), Leatherman, paracord.

Side Pocket 2:

Plastic bags, whistle, pencil sharpener, eraser, 2 pencils, pen, wipes, comb, mirror, head torch, toothbrush, toothpaste, tissue.

Expedition Leg Three: 'Bad Weather Leg'

70 litre pack with 100 litre lightweight liner inside the two cavities.

Ash Pole and Hazel pole with paracord hand loops.
Plastic trowel (attached with a clip to the pack and tucked into webbing pocket on pack).

Clothes Worn:

Mountaineering boots (half shank, leather, goretex lined), lightweight Craghopper trousers, wicking teeshirt, summer weight, 'Smartwool' socks, ankle gaiters, fleece gloves (in bumbag when not needed), paramo breathable & waterproof hat with peak and neck panel (in bumbag when not needed), watch.

Bumbag:

Compass, whistle, maps, micro towel (handkerchief-sized), water filter bottle, reading glasse, spruce resin, phone, epipen.

Main Cavity of Pack (undivided):

Poncho, triple layer goretex jacket, mountaineering mittens, waterproof trousers, technical lightweight inflating mat, micro hand towel, cacoon liner for sleeping bag (adds a season in terms of warmth), mosquito/midge face mask, charger for phone, phone charging cable, tampons, talc, all purpose biodegradable soap, insect repellant, antibacterial dry wash, cotton buds, nail file, purse (cash and card), three season sleeping bag, bivi bag, writing book, reading book, spare paper, maps not in use, filter-cleaning syring, tin can wood burner, striker (ferro rod), natural tinder, lighter, leather gloves, lightweight cooking pot and lid (mug sized), spoon (personal favourite horn spoon), pencil sharpener, eraser, 2 pencils, pen, mirror, head torch, toothbrush, toothpaste, tissue.

Bag of clothes: underwear, 2 spare pairs walking socks, Lycra shorts, spare gloves, long sleeve top, Mammut long sleeve top, Mammut short sleeve top, silk tee for sleeping, silky long johns for sleeping.

Medical/emergency kit: ibuprofen, paracetamol, diazepam (in the event of back spasms), allergy pills, tick removal tool, micropore tape, hypodermic needles, reflective squares, hydrocortisone, moleskin dressing, crepe bandage, dioralyte, wound dressings, second skin dressing, tweezers, safety pins, insect repellent, wipes, hormone tablets and patches, lymecycline for rosacea, nail file, nail clippers, lube, 6 extra head torch batteries, duct tape, string, sewing kit, scissors.

Side pockets of Pack:

Food and drinks.

Lid of Pack:

Tent pegs, head torch, knife, paracord, plastic bags (dog poo bags).

Expedition Leg Four: 'Crazy Leg'

65 litre pack with 100 litre lightweight liner inside the two cavities.
Ash pole and hazel pole with paracord hand loops.
Plastic trowel (attached with a clip to the pack).
Foraged food (hanging from bumbag or walking pole in a stuffsack).

Clothes Worn:

Walking boots made for bunions (half shank, leather, goretex lined)
Lightweight Craghopper trousers
Long sleeve Mammut top
Summer weight buff
'Smartwool' socks
Primaloft jacket
Triple layer goretex jacket (in compression pouch on pack when not needed)
Fleece gloves (in bumbag when not needed)
Paramo breathable & waterproof hat with peak and neck panel (in bumbag when not needed)
Watch

Bumbag:

Compass, whistle, maps in use, micro towel (handkerchief-sized), water filter bottle, cheap reading glasses, cheap sunglasses, phone (in waterproof tough case), epipen, vaseline.

Main Cavity of Pack (undivided):

Basha/tarp and pegs, thin foam mat, thin inflatable mat, paracord – all in a stuffsack on top of the liner.
Tough plastic bag containing pemmican portions.

In Liner:

Down duvet jacket (winter weight), mountaineering mitten, gaiters, micro hand towel, cacoon liner for sleeping bag (adds a season in terms of warmth), mosquito/midge face mask, three season sleeping bag, bivi bag.

Bag of clothes: underwear, 2 spare pairs walking socks, Lycra shorts, spare gloves, Mammut short sleeve top, silk tee for sleeping, silky long johns for sleeping.

In a lightweight waterproof stuffsack inside liner:

Charger for phone, phone charging cable and plug, purse (cash and card), spruce resin balm, tampons, talc, all purpose biodegradable soap, antibacterial dry wash, toothbrush, toothpaste, cotton buds, nail file.

Medical/emergency kit: ibuprofen, paracetamol, diazepam (in the event of back spasms), allergy pills, additional epipen, tick removal tool, micropore tape, hypodermic needles, reflective squares, hydrocortisone, crepe bandage, dioralyte, hydrocolloid plasters, wound dressings, tweezers, safety pins, insect repellent, wipes, hormone tablets and patches, lymecycline for rosacea, nail file, 6 extra head torch batteries, duct tape, string, sewing kit, folding scissors.

Tiny emergency tin with: fishing line, fishing weights, scalpel, water purification tabs, 2 waterproof matches, emery board/striking board, saw blade, iodine.

Inner pocket of main cavity

Writing book, maps not in us, 2 strong plastic bags, pencil sharpener, eraser, 2 pencils, extra pen.

Belt strap pockets:

Daily ration of: sauerkraut (in watertight beaker), fruit and nuts (in a bag), pemmican (in a bag).

Hydration pouch section inside back of pack:

Sauerkraut storage pouches (later moved to top of pack with pemmy storage bag).

Compression pouch on front of pack:

Waterproof trousers, jackets not being worn.

Left main pocket:

Nuts and fruit storage bag, filter-cleaning syringe, one spare water pouch, one spare small water pouch for clean water or sauerkraut juice.
Lightweight cooking pot and lid (mug sized), containing tea bags and coffee.
Spoon (personal favourite horn spoon).

Right main pocket:

Stove, pot, tinder, tin can wood burner, striker (small ferro rod), natural tinder, emergency waterproof matches, leather gloves.

Lid of Pack:

Collected firewood, headtorch, knife, extra paracord, plastic bags (dog poo bags), insect repellent, whisky.

Appendix Three: Expedition Data

Leg One: Trial Leg, Ditton Priors to Penkridge

Day 1. Ditton Priors to 'Bird's Green, via 'No Man's Green'.
    Thistle Field Bivi
Day 2. Bird's Green to Oak Tree Bivi
Day 3. Oak Tree Bivi to Penkridge

Mileage = 40 miles
Ascent Approx 400m (1,312ft)

Leg Two: Sickness Leg, Penkridge to Hawes

Day 1. (13.04.2015) Penkridge to Bishton. Jungle Bivi. 12m
Day 2. Bishton – Sedsall (Eaton Dovedale).
    Fallow Field Bivi. 18m
Day 3. Sedsall – Coldwall (side of river valley).
    Moss Bed Bivi. 9m
Day 4. Coldwall – Alstonefield. 'Tidy Camp' Site. 5m
Day 5. Alstonefield – Chee Dale. Clifftop Bivi. 13m
Day 6. Chee Dale – Edale. 'Dysentery Camp' Site. 13m
Day 7. Rest (sickness). Heavy rain
Day 8. Edale – Crowden Valley side. Comfort Bivi. 13m
Day 9. Crowden Valley – Wessenden Moor. Hunted Bivi. 9m
Day 10. Wessenden Moor – Mankinholes.
    YHA 'Bricks and Mortar'. 14m
Day 11. Mankinholes – Bare Hill. Rockpit Bivi. 17m
Day 12. Bare Hill – Woods north of Gargrave (via Earby).
    Pheasant Bivi 17m
Day 13. Gargrave woods – Malham Tarn. Secret Bivi. 9m
Day 14. Malham Tarn – Old Ing Moor (forest).
    Protection Bivi. 14m
Day 15. Old Ing Moor – Hawes. YHA 11m

Total Mileage = 174m
Ascent from Penkridge to the Pennine Way
    – approx 1,000m (3,280ft)

Ascent on Pennine Way to Hawes – 3,109m (10,200ft)
Total Ascent = 4,109m (13,480ft)

Leg Three: Bad Weather Leg, Hawes to the Cheviots

Day 1. (02.09.2016) Hawes to Thwaite.
　　　First Night Bivi. 10m
Day 2. Thwaite to Gods Bridge, nr Bowes.
　　　God's Bridge Bivi. 13m
Day 3. God's Bridge to Tees Valley, nr M-in-Teesdale.
　　　Hazel Tree Bivi. 11m.
Day 4. Hazel Tree Bivi to Peeping Hill, nr Dufton.
　　　Desperate Bivi. 18m
Day 5. Dufton to Greg's Hut on Cross Fell. 10m
Day 6. Greg's Hut to Larchet Hill. Makey-Do Bivi. 19m
Day 7. Larchet Hill to Peel. Mindful Bivi. 17m
Day 8. Peel to Highstead Hill, nr Bellingham.
　　　Tepee Bivi. 17m
Day 9. Highstead Hill to Border Fence, Cheviots.
　　　Border Bivi. 19m

Total Mileage = 134 Miles
Ascent = 3,450m (11,320ft)

Leg Four: Crazy Leg, Byrness to Inverie, Knoydart

Day 1. (13.04.2017) Border fence,
　　　Cheviots to Chew Green. Maundy Thursday Bivi
Day 2. Chew Green to Black Hag. Good Friday Bivi
Day 3. Black Hag to Wether Hill. Fat Burning Bivi
Day 4. Morebattle to Dere Street. Easter Sunday Bivi
Day 5. Dere Street to Gala Hill. Beauty Spot Bivi
Day 6. Galashiels to Elibank and Traquair Forest.
　　　Dugout Bivi

Day 7. Inverleithen to Kilnubie Hill. Fir Tree Bivi

Day 8. Fir Tree Bivi to A70. Mucky Night Bivi

Day 9. A70 to Union Canal, east of Linlithgow.
     Railway Line Bivi

Day 10. Linlithgow to Forth and Clyde Canal.
     Authincioch. Wild West Bivi

Day 11. Wild West Bivi to Baldernock, Milngavie.
     Laurel Nest Bivi

Day 12. Milngavie to Conic Hill.

Day 13. Conic Hill to Loch Lomond, nr Cailness.
     Rabbit Den Bivi

Day 14. Cailness to Crainlarich. Craggy Bivi

Day 15. Crainlarich to Loch Tulla. Druim a Bhtair.
     Cuckoo Bivi

Day 16. Loch Tulla to Kinlochleven. Grass Bed Bivi

Day 17. Kinlochleven to Camusnagaul. Primordial Bivi

Day 18. Camusnagaul to Glenfinnan. Wallpit Bivi

Day 19. Glenfinnan to Glen Dessary. May Day Bivi

Day 20. Glen Dessary to Sourlies Bothy.

Day 21. Sourlies Bothy to Inverie. Glitter Beach Bivi

Total Mileage = 320m

Ascent = 5,600m (18,500ft)